GRADES 3-6

DISCOVERING
WORLD CULTURES
THROUGH
LITERATURE

DISCOVERING
WORLD CULTURES
THROUGH
LITERATURE

Gerry Edwards, Ph.D

GoodYearBooks

An Imprint of ScottForesman
A Division of HarperCollinsPublishers

Dedication

To the children of the
South Manor School District
for their help in making
this book possible.

GoodYearBooks

are available for most basic curriculum subjects plus many enrichment areas.
For more GoodYearBooks, contact your local bookseller or educational dealer.
For a complete catalog with information about other GoodYearBooks, please
write:

GoodYearBooks
ScottForesman
1900 East Lake Avenue
Glenview, IL 60025

Book design by Street Level Studio.
Illustrated by Yoshi Miyake.
Copyright © 1995 Gerry Edwards.
All Rights Reserved.
Printed in the United States of America.

ISBN 0-673-36130-6

1 2 3 4 5 6 7 8 9 - ER - 02 01 00 99 98 97 96 95 94

Contents

Part Two: The Earth's Elements

Unit Seven: Land

Unit Eight: People of the World

Unit Nine: Sun and Moon

Unit Ten: Wind and Water

Unit Eleven: Perspectives for World Environments and Cultures

Bibliography

Introduction

Learning to care and appreciate the wonders and mysteries of our natural world in relationship to human culture is crucial to the purpose of this book. Encouraging educators, parents, and children to become involved in the study of world environments and cultures is a first step to securing the very delicate bond that exists between humans and their natural world.

This book has three objectives. The first is to offer educators and parents an interdisciplinary, holistic, and literature-based approach to the teaching of world environments and cultures. The second objective is to promote a sensitivity to environmental processes, issues, and concerns, and to explore the possible challenges facing specific environments and cultures around the world. The third objective is to provide a multicultural perspective, rooted in diversity, interdependency, and respect, which will enable children to perceive themselves as a small part of a global community.

Part One of this book offers interdisciplinary themes that allow children to explore world environments and cultures. Each theme is preceded by a reading activity. Teachers should read the activity to their students as an introduction to a specific theme. A discussion section and questions follow each reading. Interdisciplinary activities enhance each theme's objectives. For example, students will hear the sounds of a rain forest, visit a desert cactus hotel, get to know the mountain people of Appalachia, and witness an Arctic oil spill. Each environment gives life to new and different cultures. The people of each region, although different in their specific beliefs and practices, are similar in their daily struggle to meet the needs of human survival.

Many of the interdisciplinary activities will stimulate children to use their senses while studying the dynamics of world environments and cultures. Children will be able to see an eagle in flight, feel a big bear's fur, smell a skunk's scent, hear a raven's cry, or taste a sea's breeze. These sensory images will allow children to further understand the animals and people of the world.

Children will be intrigued by the environmental and cultural activities that encourage them to explore the challenges facing today's world environments and cultures. They will study, for example, Eskimo hunters, coal miners of Pennsylvania, Yanomamo hunter/gatherers of the rain forest, and farmers tilling the world's soil. Each cultural activity lends insight into the beliefs and practices of a distinct group, as well as a better understanding into how these cultures are fighting to survive the drastic changes taking place daily within their environmental settings.

For most world cultures, change through the process of adaptation is the only way to secure survival. The more cultures students explore, the more likely they are to pick up on the general trends of change facing many of these cultures. Some of these trends include:

1) movement from the extended family to the nuclear family;

2) competitive economic practices versus cooperative practices;

3) year-round settlement versus seasonal settlement;

4) greater emphasis on wage-earning activities as opposed to traditional economic practices;

5) greater family mobility;

6) increase in the presence of women in the public work force; and

7) political subordination to larger, more powerful, foreign cultures.

The integration of the above trends produces cultural adaptations that are unique to the specific culture being studied.

All themes in Part One invite students to learn, care, and respect the world's natural environments. Many of the cultures they will research have long traditions of equality, unity, and oneness with nature. On the other hand, most of these traditional cultures, like the environments they depend on, are changing at such a rapid pace that the traditional respect for nature competes with human survival. Our children must learn to respect nature and understand the crucial role it plays in their lives.

Part Two of this book focuses on the earth's elements, and how each is crucial to the preservation of all world cultures. Students will enjoy celebrating sunrise around the world, exploring the seasonal cycle of the thirteen moons on the back of a turtle, learning about the earth's water cycle, tracing the world's wind patterns, and visiting Joe McCrephy's abandoned cornfield somewhere in Ohio.

Like Part One, each theme is introduced with a reading activity, followed by questions and discussion. The interdisciplinary activities are designed to encourage children to gain understanding and respect for the partnership that must exist between nature and humanity in order for both to survive. Students will begin their journey to better understanding this dynamic partnership by following the moon through its phases, recording the daily activities of the sun, illustrating the water cycle, and exploring the different types of wind around the world.

Many activities in both Parts One and Two of this book are focused around stories gene-rated by world cultures to explain the mysteries and wonders of nature. Drylongso, for example, is an African American folk hero who helps save a small family from the devastation of a drought in a farming community somewhere west of the Mississippi. The Maasai, who live in the grasslands of Kenya and Tanzania, tell a beautiful story about

how the planet Venus helped save an old Maasai man from starving by turning into an orphan boy. Crow and Weasel, personified as Native American characters, travel beyond their culture to lands and people unknown to them. As they travel, they gain a respect for cultural diversity, and learn the human obligation to help and care about people from all lands.

Learning about world environments and cultures will lead you and your students into many discussions about the issues and concerns of environmental and cultural change around the world. These issues and concerns are given a great deal of attention throughout the entire book. For example, students will observe a cornfield for fifty years and watch it grow into a forest. They will look through a child's bedroom window at the wilderness outside, and watch it change over the years into a scene of many houses, stores, and automobiles. They will study cultures coming into contact with other cultures, and analyze the challenges inherent in a "contact environment."

The final unit of this book is dedicated to exploring environmental perspectives that will reflect a concern and reverence for the mutually dependent relationship between world environments and cultures. Students address the issues relating to endangered environments and cultures. They will learn about the animals and people who are endangered and how they can help make a difference in preserving these environments and cultures. Teaching children to appreciate and respect the diversity of human behavior in relation to environmental settings is one of the greatest gifts we can give to them. It allows them to see beyond themselves, and to accept the many different ways people around the world organize their lives to fulfill the basic survival needs we all share.

Learning to revere ourselves in relation to other world cultures is the first step in securing global understanding and survival. Perhaps the story of Miss Rumphius, who took her grandfather's advice to try and make the world more beautiful, is one of the best examples of teaching children the importance of seeking visions that allow them to feel that they can really make a difference in today's world, as well as tomorrow's future. Like Miss Rumphius, we should try and create educational visions that celebrate learning and caring about the earth that gives us all life. This book is a small contribution to the belief that our visions can come true.

Rumblings in the Rain Forest

Introduction

For centuries the anteaters, macaws, and butterflies of the world's rain forests have lived peacefully in an environment of exotic beauty and diversity. Suddenly the animals of the rain forests hear a new sound—the sound of machines cutting down their forest. It begins to rain and the forest floods. The trees that held the soil in place are gone. The animals flee to safety, but how long can they remain safe? What will happen when the mighty machines return?

This theme will focus on the adaptations creatures of the rain forests needed to make in response to human intervention of their habitats.

Reading Activity

Rain Forest

by Helen Cowcher (Farrar Straus and Giroux, 1988)

Questions

1. What is the cry of alarm that sounds through the rain forest?
2. Why are machines cutting the trees of the rain forest down?
3. What happens to animals of the rain forest when the rains come?
4. What do you think the animals fear most?
5. Why did the author write this story and how does it relate to our lives?

Outcomes

1. To develop an awareness of how human intervention has disrupted the ecosystem of many rain forests around the world
2. To appreciate how animals within a specific ecosystem have adapted to human intervention

Materials

- "Animals of the Rain Forest" worksheet
- *Rain Forest Secrets* by Arthur Dorros. Scholastic, 1990. (optional)

Discussion

A rain forest is a lush environment where animal and plant life are plentiful. Within this environment, different animals make their homes in the diverse stratum provided by the rain forest. Macaws and hummingbirds reside in the sunlight of the rain forest's canopy, while chimpanzees and mandrills inhabit the damp and dark forest floor.

Using the worksheet titled "Animals of the Rain Forest," have students develop an outline of rain forest animals showing where they live within the ecosystem of the rain forest. The book *Rain Forest Secrets* by Arthur Dorros might prove a helpful resource to students involved in this activity.

When outlines are completed, have the class discuss how the animals of each stratum utilize their environmental niche, and how human intervention has threatened to endanger all levels of animal life within the rain forest.

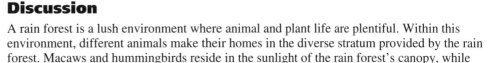

Interdisciplinary Activities

Activity 1 — From an Animal's Perspective

Introduction

The needs of animals living in the rain forests of the world often conflict with the needs of the human populations surrounding them. This activity will explore what animals might say about the changes in their habitats, if given a voice to speak.

Outcomes

1. To create an animal's point of view of environmental change through the literary strategy of personification.
2. To recognize and respect the importance of "point of view" when making environmental decisions.

Materials

- *Wolf's Version of The Three Little Pigs* by A. Wolf
- composition paper
- reference materials
- "From an Animal's Perspective" worksheet

Procedure

1. Read the book *Wolf's Version of The Three Little Pigs* to the class. Discuss the importance of point of view in any decision-making process. Focus on points of view that might be particularly relevant to environmental decision-making as it applies to global rain forests.

2. As a class, make a list of animals who live in a rain forest. Have each student select a favorite rain forest animal and research its physical and social characteristics relative to its changing environment.

3. When students have completed this task, they are ready to begin a writing assignment discussing environmental changes in the rain forest from their animal's point of view. The worksheet titled "From an Animal's Perspective" can be used to help students complete this assignment.

4. The class can share their stories in an effort to understand how human decision-making policy is altering the lives of many diverse animal populations.

Extending the Theme

• Write a play about the changing world of the rain forests from an animal's point of view.

• Create a rain forest bookmark.

• • • • • • • • • • • • • • •

| Activity 2 | A Tropical Rain Forest: Before and After Human Intervention |

Introduction

A tropical rain forest provides a variety of environments for the many animals who call it home. While some animals reside in its canopy, other animals choose its dark forest floor. This activity will ask students to produce a stratified illustration of a rain forest before and after human intervention.

Outcomes

1. To demonstrate through illustration the stratification of a rain forest
2. To create an awareness of how rain forests are changing in response to human intervention

Materials

• photos of rain forests
• drawing paper
• markers
• "Tropical Rain Forests Before and After Human Intervention" worksheet

Procedure

1. Provide the class with pictures of tropical rain forests before human intervention. Discuss the diverse plant and animal habitats of the rain forest. Provide the class with a picture of a tropical rain forest after human intervention. What changes have taken place?

2. Using the "Tropical Rain Forests Before and After Human Intervention" worksheet, culminate the discussion by having students draw two illustrations. Their first illustration should represent a tropical rain forest before human intervention and the second should portray it after. Encourage students to show the diverse strata of the rain forest in their illustrations.

Extending the Theme

• Organize a "Saving Our Rain Forests" poster contest for your classroom. Winners can be given a free homework pass, an environmental bookmark, or a pencil.

• Plan a classroom party which features foods of the rain forest. Add atmosphere to the party by providing a musical recording of the sounds of the rain forest.

Name: _____ **Date:** _____

Animals of the Rain Forest

A. Canopy

1. _____

2. _____

3. _____

4. _____

5. _____

B. Middle Level

1. _____

2. _____

3. _____

4. _____

5. _____

C. Forest Level

1. _____

2. _____

3. _____

4. _____

5. _____

Name:_____ **Date:**_____

From an Animal's Perspective

You are a rain forest animal. Give your point of view concerning the changes taking place in your environment.

Animal:_____

Point of View:_____

_____

_____

_____

_____

_____

_____

From *Discovering World Cultures Through Literature* published by GoodYearBooks. Copyright © 1995 Gerry Edwards.

Tropical Rain Forest Before and After Human Intervention

Describe and illustrate a tropical rain forest before human intervention.

_____

_____

_____

Describe and illustrate a tropical rain forest after human intervention.

_____

_____

_____

Introduction

The Daintree Rain Forest is part of a wilderness that stretches between the Daintree River and Bloomfield in North Queensland, Australia. Although the largest pristine rain forest remaining in Australia, it is faced with drastic changes that threaten its survival.

This theme explores the beauty and exotic wonders of the rain forest through the experience of a young boy. As he walks through the forest, he discovers its magic; a magic created by meandering vines, intricately twisted trees, and abundantly colorful plant and animal life. At his journey's end, he is forced to think about the future of the rain forest and to wonder how long it can remain a pristine environment in the wake of such devastating change.

Reading Activity

Where the Forest Meets the Sea

by Jeannie Baker (Greenwillow, 1978)

Questions

1. During his walk into the Daintree Rain Forest, the main character, a young boy, tried to pretend it was 100 million years earlier. Why did he want to go back in time?

2. What ancient animals did he find in the rain forest that were there 100 million years ago but are extinct today?

3. How did the author of the story perceive the future of the Daintree Rain Forest?

4. What was the name of the boat the young boy and his father used to get to the rain forest and how is the name meaningful to the future of the rain forest?

5. What do you think children around the world can do to save the pristine environment of the tropical rain forests?

Outcomes

1. To inspire children to appreciate the natural and exotic beauty of a tropical rain forest

2. To develop a concern and respect for the survival of the rain forests in Australia and throughout the world

Materials

- "Rain Forests: Then and Now" worksheet
- reference materials
- pencil

Discussion

Many plants and animals of the ancient rain forests have become extinct. Ask students to think about the changes in the environment that made it impossible for them to survive. What changes are occurring in today's rain forests and how are they endangering specific plant and animal populations? Discuss what people can do to make a difference in preserving the plant and animal life of rain forests around the world.

Using the "Rain Forests: Then and Now" worksheet, ask students to chart the similarities and differences of today's rain forests with the rain forests of 100 million years ago.

Culminate the lesson by having students respond to the question on the same worksheet which asks "How can you help to save the rain forests of the world?" Ask students to share their responses with their classmates.

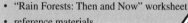

Interdisciplinary Activities

Activity 1   A Walk in the Rain Forest

Introduction

Exploring the natural world around us with someone special can be a great way to spend a vacation, weekend, or even a day. Such an exploration provides us with the opportunity to step back from our daily routines and share in the beauty and magnificence of nature.

Outcomes

1. To encourage children to learn about the geography of their natural environment through participation and observation
2. To develop an awareness of the environment through the sharing of it with others

Materials

- composition paper
- pencils
- photos or illustrations of rain forests
- "A Walk in a Rain Forest" worksheet

Procedure

1. Encourage students to recall a time that they spent in a natural surrounding with a friend or relative. What made the adventure into nature unique and important? How did it compare to the experience of the young boy in the story *Where the Forest Meets the Sea?*

2. Using illustrations of diverse rain forests, have the class try to imagine a walk into the forest with a special friend. Distribute the worksheet "A Walk in a Rain Forest" and ask students to write what they would see, feel, and learn as part of their journey. Follow-up the writing assignment by having them illustrate their favorite rain forest scene.

3. Encourage children to read and discuss their stories as experiences that inspired bonding between people and the natural world that unites them.

Extending the Theme

- Plan a field trip to a local park or nature preserve. Take a nature walk. Record the sights, smells, and sounds you encounter during your visit.

- Write a letter to the Australian Consulate requesting information about the rain forests of Australia.

• • • • • • • • • • • • • • •

Activity 2 Rain Forest Collage

Introduction

The featured author of this theme, Jeannie Baker, illustrates her story through an artistic composition known as a collage. Children will enjoy creating their own versions of a rain forest by sharing Jeannie Baker's illustrative style.

Outcomes

1. To create a collage which illustrates a rain forest
2. To develop an appreciation of rain forests through artistic expression

Materials

- white or brown rolled paper
- markers
- crayons
- modeling clay
- textured and natural materials
- *Where the Forest Meets the Sea* by Jeannie Baker
- "Rain Forest Collage" worksheet

Procedure

1. Review Baker's rain forest illustrations as examples of an art form artists refer to as collage. Encourage them to think about ways they, as a class, can create a rain forest collage.

2. Break the class up into groups of two or three students. Using the "Rain Forest Collage" worksheet, ask each group to choose one rain forest landscape that they will contribute to the final collage. After they have made their decision as a group, they should begin planning for the materials they will need and the procedure they will follow in creating their collage. They might want to do a small practice illustration using the space provided on the worksheet.

3. Use brown or white rolled paper to do the final class collage. The paper should be divided into sections so that members of each group can work cooperatively in producing the final collage.

Extending the Theme

- Write a composition explaining your rain forest collage.

- Research and discuss how artists use collage to express their feelings about the world surrounding them. How can we use the work provided by artists to save our natural environments?

From *Discovering World Cultures Through Literature* published by GoodYearBooks. Copyright © 1995 Gerry Edwards.

Name: ______________________ **Date:** ______________

Rain Forests: Then and Now

Compare the similarities and differences between the ancient rain forests and the rain forests of today.

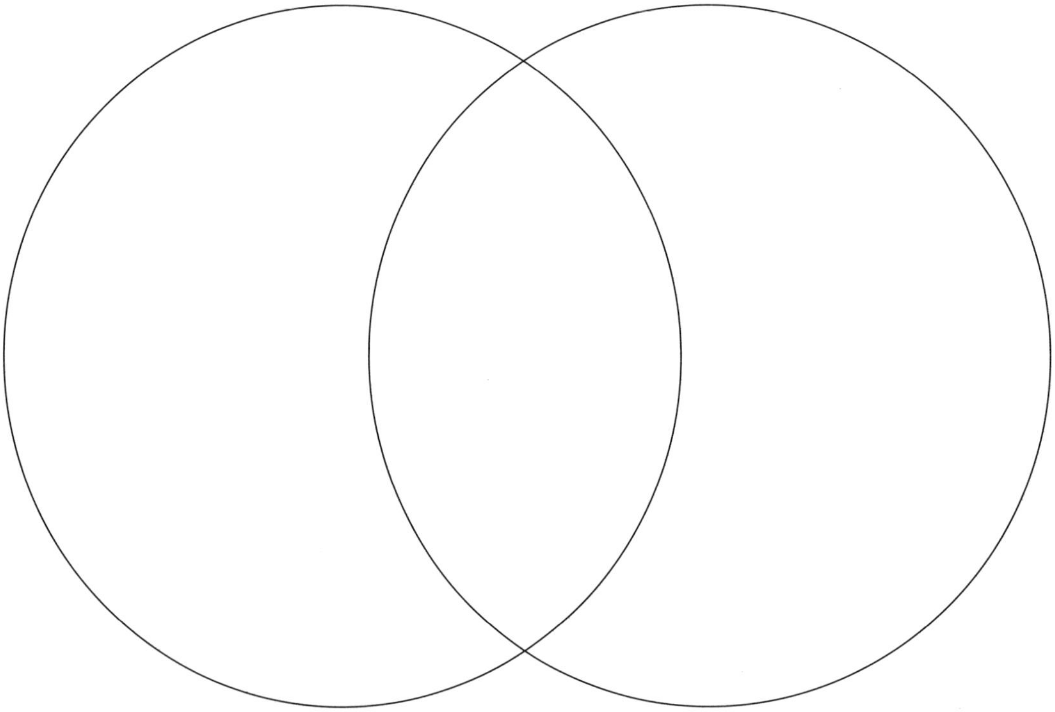

Ancient Rain Forests

Contemporary Rain Forests

Question: How can you help save the world's rain forests?

Response: ____

____

____

____

____

Name: _____ **Date:** _____

A Walk in the Rain Forest

You and a special friend are taking a walk in a rain forest. Describe what you see and hear as you explore the secrets of this very unique environment.

_____

_____

_____

_____

_____

Illustrate your favorite rain forest landscape.

Rain Forest Collage

Group Participants

Rain Forest Scene

Materials

Procedure

Illustration

Introduction

When we think of a rain forest, most of us think of a tropical rain forest. There are, however, other types of rain forests around the world that provide a rich and abundant environment for many different plant, animal, and human populations. Scientists believe that there are over thirty million kinds of plants and animals living on the earth. Half of them are thought to live in the rain forests of the world. This is very interesting since rain forests only cover a small amount of the earth. This theme will explore the secrets of the rain forests, and how we can keep these very precious secrets alive.

Reading Activity

Rain Forest Secrets

by Arthur Dorros (Scholastic Inc., 1990)

Questions

1. What are the three layers of a rain forest?
2. What are the different types of rain forests found around the world?
3. What kinds of plants found in rain forests are used as food by human populations?
4. How have specific plants found in the rain forest been useful in curing disease?
5. Why did the author title this book *Rain Forest Secrets?*

Outcomes

1. To appreciate the diversity of rain forests around the world
2. To gain an understanding of how rain forests have provided the necessary resources for the survival of many plant, animal, and human populations

Materials

• outline of a world map
• "Rain Forests of the World" worksheet
• pencil

Discussion

The author Arthur Dorros explores three different types of rain forests in his book, *Rain Forest Secrets.* He also provides an illustrated map showing the locations of the world's rain forests. Using the author's map as a guide, provide students with an outline of a world map (refer to the worksheet titled "Rain Forests of the World"), and ask them to plot the different types of rain forests in their geographical locations.

Once students have completed their maps, compare and contrast the three types of rain forests. Questions to be addressed should include:

1. Are three layers found in all types of rain forests?
2. What similar and different plants and animals can be found in each rain forest?
3. Why are all rain forests so important to people everywhere in the world?

Interdisciplinary Activities

Activity 1 **People of the Rain Forest**

Introduction

People living in a rain forest have particular lifestyles dependent on the environment which surrounds them. Your class can begin exploring these unique lifestyles by investigating several of the traditional cultures of the rain forests around the world. Examples include the Mundurucu of Brazil, the Yucatán Maya of Mexico, the Yanomamo of Venezuela, and the Pygmies of the Belgian Congo (Africa).

Outcomes

1. To investigate and analyze traditional cultures of specific rain forests in their changing environments
2. To gain an appreciation and understanding for the interdependence of geography and culture

Materials

- "People of the Rain Forest" worksheet
- reference materials specific to cultures being studied

Procedure

1. Begin the activity by discussing with your class what the word *culture* means. (The arts, beliefs, customs, institutions, and all other products of human work and thought created by a people or group at a particular time. *The American Heritage Dictionary*. Dell, 1983.)

2. Have each student choose a traditional rain forest culture and investigate its economy, government, family organization, geography, and religion. Use the "People of the Rain Forest" worksheet to help students record the necessary information.

3. While gathering data, your class will soon realize that many of these traditional cultures have changed significantly due to the same exploitation the plants and animals have experienced. When students have completed their charts, have the class come together to discuss traditional cultures of the rain forests and how the forces of change have altered their lifestyles.

Extending the Theme

- Write an illustrated ethnography (description) of a traditional rain forest culture. Use your "Before-After" chart as an outline to help you write.

- Investigate how various plants of the rain forest have been used in curing disease around the world.

- - - - - - - - - - - - - -

Activity 2 Rain Forest Trivia

Introduction

The magnitude of plant and animal life in the rain forests of the world make it an ideal topic for a student-generated trivia game. Your class will enjoy gathering information and designing a trivia game that can be shared with classmates and friends at home and in school.

Outcomes

1. To have students gather and organize information into a meaningful classification system
2. To develop a trivia game based on the classification system generated from research

Materials

- "Rain Forest Trivia" worksheet
- reference materials (refer to Rain Forest bibliography)
- oaktag
- cardboard
- markers
- index cards
- dice

Procedure

1. Organize students into cooperative groups. Assign each group a rain forest in one of the following regions: North America, South America, Central America, Africa, Asia, or Australia.

2. Each group should collect information for their regional rain forest and record it on the worksheet titled "Rain Forest Trivia." Once they have listed trivia for several different categories, they should organize it into a Rain Forest Trivia card or board game.

3. When all groups have completed the assignment, they can compare and contrast the information they collected by sharing their Rain Forest Trivia games.

Extending the Theme

- Plan a vacation to a tropical rain forest. Which one would you like to visit? How would you get there? What would you take with you? What would you want to do or see while visiting? What do you think you would enjoy the most about your visit? What do you think you would like the least?

- Pretend you are a child living in a rain forest. Write about how you think your make-believe life would be different than your real life. How would it be the same?

Name: _____ **Date:** _____

Rain Forests of the World

Use the map outline below to plot the geographical locations of the major rain forests around the world. Create a map key to distinguish between the different types of rain forests.

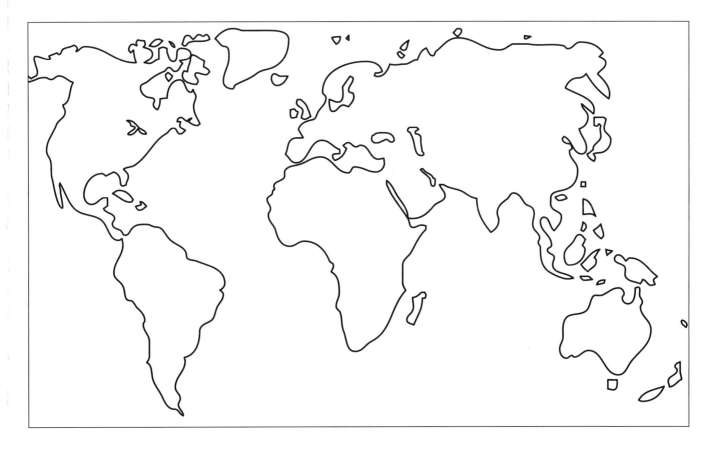

Key:

Name: _____ **Date:** _____

People of the Rain Forest

Choose a traditional rain forest culture and record pre-exploitation and post-exploitation data for the cultural categories listed.

Culture	Pre-exploitation	Post-exploitation
Geography		
Plants/Animals		
Family Organization		
Government		
Beliefs/Rituals		
Customs		

Rain Forest Trivia

Name of Rain Forest

Location

Canopy Trivia

Middle Level Trivia

Forest Floor Trivia

Endangered Species Trivia

People of the Forest Trivia

World Rain Forests Trivia

The Baobab Tree: A Mother to the African Savannahs

Introduction

The African people of the dry savannahs refer to the baobab tree as "mother." This revered tree of massive proportions (40 feet across, 60 feet in height) provides shelter and food to an enormous array of wildlife. It also provides the African people with fruit and honey, along with bark for their baskets and roots for their medicines.

Exploring the ecosystem of the African savannahs through the story of the baobab tree will encourage children to develop an insight into the cycle of this tree and the plant and animal life it helps to support. Once students can appreciate the importance of the baobab tree to the African savannah, they will truly begin to understand why this tree is called "the tree of life."

Reading Activity

Tree of Life

by Barbara Bash (Sierra Club Books and Little, Brown & Company, 1989)

Questions

1. What is the legend behind the baobab tree and how did this legend influence the tree's appearance?
2. Why do the African people refer to the baobab tree as "mother"?
3. How does the baobab tree remind you of your mother?
4. What forms of life does the baobab tree help to support?
5. How do you think your life would be different if you lived in an African savannah?

Outcomes

1. To explore the ecosystem of the African savannah through the life cycle of the baobab tree
2. To gain an awareness of the interdependent relationships that exist between the baobab tree and the various forms of life it supports

Materials

- Life Cycle of a Baobab Tree" worksheet
- pencil

Discussion

Have students develop a sequential diagram to illustrate the life cycle of the baobab tree. Use the "Life Cycle of a Baobab Tree" worksheet to complete the assignment. When worksheets are finished, have the class compare the similarities and differences between human life cycles and the life cycle of the baobab tree.

Interdisciplinary Activities

Activity 1 — The Cultural Dynamics of Motherhood

Introduction

Motherhood in many cultures, simple and complex, is associated with the transmission of cultural values. These values keep a culture alive. The role of motherhood in many societies is also associated with everyday domestic and nurturing activities (cooking, cleaning, child care).

It would also be wise to note that in some households within a culture, the role of primary nurturer is often filled by an adult guardian (father, grandparents, adoptive parents, etc.) other than a mother.

When the African Bushmen refer to the baobab tree as "mother," they are using the term to signify the importance of the baobab in preserving their traditional lifestyle.

From *Discovering World Cultures Through Literature* published by GoodYearBooks. Copyright © 1995 Gerry Edwards.

Outcomes

1. To develop the importance of the role of motherhood, cross-culturally, to the transmission of cultural values

2. To appreciate cultural stability in terms of preserving traditional cultural values

Materials

• "The Motherhood Tree" worksheet

Procedure

Like the African Bushmen, we have a concept of "motherhood" in our cultural experience. Using life experiences, have students record how their mothers or their guardians have helped them to grow from babies to fourth, fifth, or sixth graders. It is also important for children to record how they feel their mothers or their guardians will continue to nurture and guide them into adulthood. Use the "The Motherhood Tree" worksheet for this activity.

Extending the Theme

• Compare and contrast the life cycle (birth, youth, marriage, old age, death) of an American child with that of a !Kung child. (Reference: *Kalahare Hunter-Gatherers: Studies of the !Kung San and Their Neighbors* by Richard B. Lee and Irven Devore. Harvard University Press, 1976)

• Create a poem titled "Motherhood."

• • • • • • • • • • • • • • •

Activity 2   An Ethnography of the !Kung

Introduction

Environment is crucial to the lifestyle of most world cultures. The !Kung Bushmen of Africa are a prime example of how important a role the environment plays in the economic, political, and religious life of the African savannahs. Students will enjoy exploring the environment and culture through research and writing of a !Kung ethnography.

Outcomes

1. To establish an awareness of the interdependent relationship between environment and culture

2. To research and compose an ethnography about the !Kung Bushmen of the African savannahs

Materials

• encyclopedias or other reference books
• world map or globe
• paper

Procedure

1. Begin by explaining that an ethnography describes the lifestyle of a particular group of people, in this case, the !Kung Bushmen of the African savannahs. Avenues of investigation in piecing together the ethnography should include: 1) geography, 2) plant and animal life, 3) beliefs and values, 4) customs, traditions, and rituals, 5) economy, and 6) government.

2. Divide students into small groups and assign each group one of the above areas to research. When the groups have gathered all the necessary data, they should write and illustrate a two- to three- page report describing the area they researched. When all groups have completed their reports, they should be compiled into one book and titled *The !Kung Bushmen*. This ethnography will allow children to observe and critically discuss the intricate relationship between environment and culture. They might want to apply this information to their own culture.

Extending the Theme

• Create a diorama of an African savannah.

• Think about how our national flag is symbolic to our culture. Design a flag for the !Kung that reflects their culture.

Name: ______________________ **Date:** ______________

Life Cycle of Baobab Tree

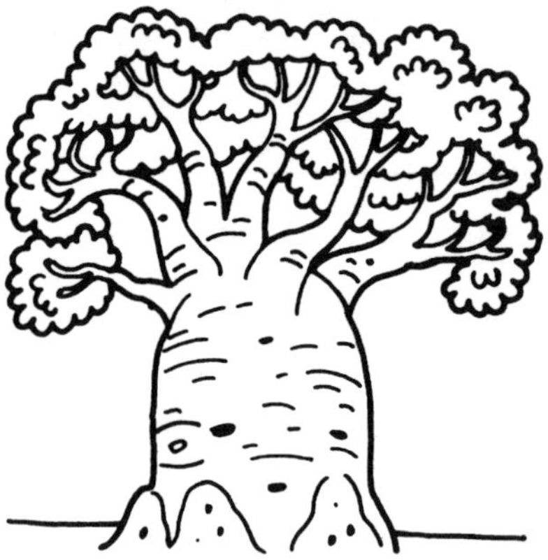

Describe the life cycle of a baobab tree.

Before the Rain

During the Rain

After the Rain

Question: How does the life cycle of the baobab tree influence the lifestyle of the people inhabiting the African savannahs?

Response: ____

____

____

____

____

Name: _____ Date: _____

The Motherhood Tree

List ways mothers or other guardians help children grow from infants to adulthood.

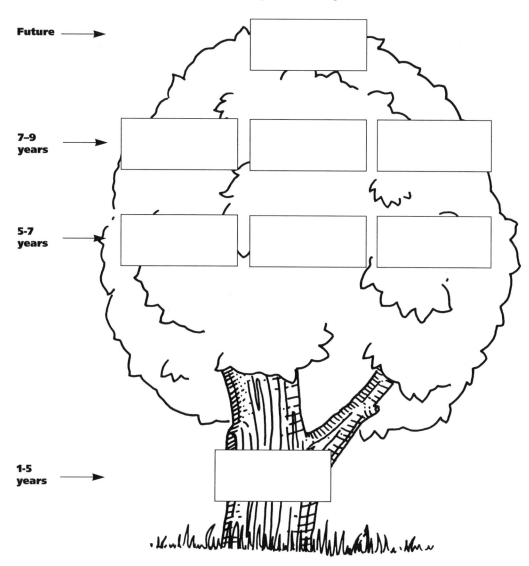

Future ⟶

7–9 years ⟶

5-7 years ⟶

1-5 years ⟶

Question: Based on the activities recorded above, how important is the role of nurturer to cultural survival?

Response: _____

_____

_____

_____

Introduction

Family farms of the United States are facing powerful obstacles in their efforts to maintain a lifestyle that is deeply rooted in America's heritage. According to the U.S. Department of Agriculture (1986), one American farm goes out of business every six minutes.

This theme will address the lifestyle and concerns of the American family farm by focusing on three very diverse farm families. Your students will meet the MacMillans of Massachusetts, who specialize in dairy farming; the Rosmanns of Iowa, who own an organic hog and grain operation; and the Adamses of Georgia, who raise chickens and belong to a newly created farm cooperative. The experiences of these families will provide insight into the challenges facing American families who choose to be the "caretakers of the land."

Reading Activity

The American Family Farm

by Joan Anderson (Harcourt Brace Jovanovich, 1989)

Questions

1. How are women and children important to the American farm family?
2. What beliefs about the land do the three families share?
3. What is the work ethic expressed by all three families?
4. What concerns for the future were shared by the MacMillans, Adamses, and Rosmanns?
5. How do the concerns of these three families relate to the concerns of all Americans?

Outcomes

1. To explore the lifestyle and concerns of the American farm family
2. To identify and analyze the technological, economic, and social change of the American farm family

Materials

- "Caretakers of the Land" worksheet
- pencil

Discussion

Joan Anderson, who wrote the text for *The American Family Farm*, communicates the beliefs and practices of American farm families to readers by using quotes from the three families studied. Have each student find two quotes from each family that reflect a belief or practice of their particular family. The final response question addresses that by listening to their beliefs, we can gain an understanding of those who "till the soil." Refer to the "Caretakers of the Land" worksheet.

Interdisciplinary Activities

Activity 1 — Understanding Culture Through Proverbs

Introduction

Proverbs are oral phrases which are passed on from generation to generation by groups who share similar cultural experiences. Proverbs tend to be very stable expressions of a cultural heritage and are, therefore, useful in studying the historical record of a geographic region, from the "folk" perspective. Such a perspective will inspire students to take a journey into America's past as well as its future.

20

From *Discovering World Cultures Through Literature* published by GoodYearBooks. Copyright © 1995 Gerry Edwards.

Outcomes

1. To identify and apply proverbs to American beliefs and lifestyles
2. To create proverbs for America's future

Materials

- "Famous American Proverbs" worksheet

Procedure

1. Discuss with the class the meaning and application of several proverbs. You might want to begin by using proverbs that are familiar to American farm families:

    a. He's as awkward as a cow with a musket. (Maine)

    b. Running around like a chicken with its head cut off. (Tennessee)

    c. Independent as a hog on ice. (New England)

    d. The world is your cow, but you have to do the milking. (New York)

    e. You can take the boy out of the country, but you can't take the country out of the boy. (Illinois).

2. Discuss with the class why the above proverbs might be particularly meaningful to farm families. Have students brainstorm a list of proverbs which are meaningful to their lifestyles. Test their knowledge of well-known American proverbs by hav ing them complete the "Famous American Proverbs" worksheet.

References:

- Emrich, Duncan. *Folklore on the American Land*. Little, Brown and Company, 1972.
- Monteiro, George. *Proverbs in the Remaking*. Western Folklore, 1968.

Extending the Theme

- Collect proverbs from different regions of the United States. Have students design flash cards by putting the first part of the proverb on one side and the second part on the opposite side. Example: You can't teach an old dog/new tricks.
- Create new proverbs which express truths of today's America. Examples might include experiences relating to anything from computers to space travel.

• • • • • • • • • • • • • • •

Activity 2 The Seasonal Cycle of Farming

Introduction

Life on a farm is dictated by a seasonal cycle. There is a time to plant and a time to harvest; a time to milk the cows, a time to sell the cows; a time to work and a time to play. The three families studied in the book all focus their daily routines around a seasonal clock. Exploring the seasonal clock of the MacMillans, the Adamses, and the Rosmanns will provide students with an opportunity to compare the importance of seasonal activity to lifestyle.

Outcomes

1. To provide an awareness of the relationship of seasonal activity to lifestyle
2. To inspire students to appreciate diverse lifestyles

Materials

- "Seasonal Clocks of Culture" worksheet

Procedure

Discuss time and season by comparing the four seasons of the year to the four quarters of a clock. Refer to the "Seasonal Clocks of Culture" worksheet. Students should take one of the families researched by Anderson and fill in the appropriate clock. The second clock is filled in with activities that reflect their seasonal cycle. Follow up the activity with a discussion that compares and contrasts the two cultural clocks.

Extending the Theme

- Choose a regional or occupational lifestyle and illustrate its seasonal clock.
- Research how technology has changed the lifestyle of the American farmer. Record the changes on a timeline.

Name: _____ **Date:** _____

Caretakers of the Land

Identify two quotes from each family that reflect a belief or practice of their particular family.

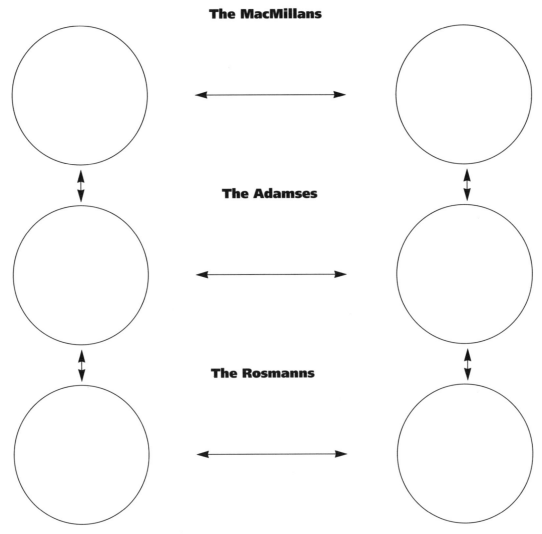

The MacMillans

The Adamses

The Rosmanns

Question: How are all the above quotes linked to understanding the lifestyle of America's family farms?

Response: _____

_____

_____

_____

_____

From *Discovering World Cultures Through Literature* published by GoodYearBooks. Copyright © 1995 Gerry Edwards.

Famous American Proverbs

1. Spare the rod and _____ .

2. Man does not live by _____ .

3. Two heads are_____ .

4. The pen is mightier than_____ .

5. Half a loaf is better than _____ .

6. You can't gct blood out of a _____ .

7. Ask me no questions and I'll tell you_____ .

8. Sly as a_____ .

9. Stubborn as a _____ .

10. Snug as a bug in a_____ .

11. Looks like something the cat _____ .

12. Better late than_____ .

13. You can lead a horse to water, but _____

_____ .

Seasonal Clocks of Culture

Compare your seasonal activities with those of a farm family.

Student

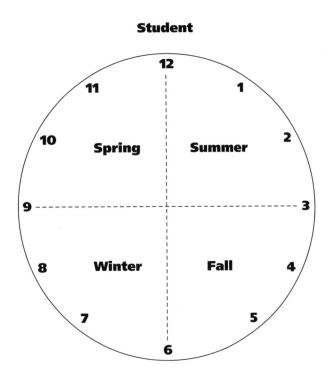

Farm Family

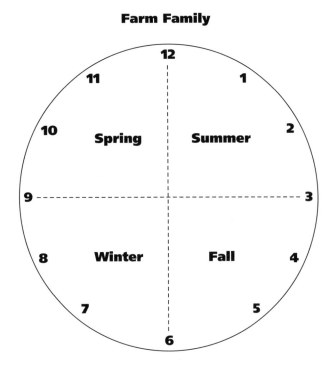

Question: How are the above two seasonal clocks similar? How are they different?

Response: _____

_____

_____

_____

_____

The Maasai and the Orphan Boy

Introduction

Many cultures of the world believe that their daily activities are connected and affected by mysterious occurrences within the universe. This relationship between humans and celestial bodies is often expressed by people in myths, legends, and folk tales.

This theme will focus on a legend told by a pastoral people known as the Maasai. The Maasai inhabit the grasslands of Kenya and Tanzania, and their story provides us with a very beautiful explanation about how the planet Venus helped to save an old Maasai man by turning into an orphan boy. It is a very powerful tale of people and nature working together.

Reading Activity

The Orphan Boy

by Tololwa M. Mollel (Clarion Books, 1990)

Questions

1. How did the old man welcome Kileken, the orphan boy?
2. How did Kileken help the old man?
3. What did Kileken do to make the old man suspicious of him?
4. What did the old man's shadow tell him to do?
5. What was Kileken's secret and why is he called the orphan boy?

Outcomes

1. To introduce the relationship between human and celestial bodies through folklore
2. To analyze and understand the Maasai people of the African grasslands through the legend of *The Orphan Boy*

Materials

- "The Old Man and the Orphan Boy" worksheet
- pencil

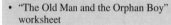

Discussion

Legends are stories respected by their tellers as true. They usually take place in secular settings and portray human characters within historical situations. All cultures create legends and most of these legends become part of the oral tradition passed down from generation to generation. Like most stories, legends have a setting, a problem, and a resolution. Using the "The Old Man and the Orphan Boy" worksheet, discuss the setting, problem, and events leading to the final resolution of this Maasai legend.

Interdisciplinary Activities

Activity 1 Wishing Upon a Star

Introduction

The beauty of a starlit sky belongs to all people inhabiting the earth. As we share in that beauty, many of us experience the same feelings of solitude, tranquillity, and harmony with the unknown. We may also occasionally make a wish upon a star in the hope of bringing happiness to ourselves or someone we love. Maybe our wish, like that of the old Maasai man, will bring us prosperity and good fortune.

Outcomes

1. To appreciate a starlit sky as a source of beauty and inspiration to all cultures of the world
2. To develop an awareness and respect for the relationship between humans and celestial bodies

Materials

- "Wishing Upon a Star" worksheet

Procedure

1. Encourage students to recall a "stargazing" experience they shared with a friend or relative. What was special about their evening with the stars? What did they learn about the stars relative to the sun, moon, and planets? How did their experience compare with that of the old Maasai man and the orphan boy?

2. Have students close their eyes and pretend they are stargazing. Ask each child to contemplate five wishes they would make and how these wishes would change their lives. Use the "Wishing Upon a Star" worksheet to write down the five wishes. When the class has completed assignment, discuss the worksheets in the context of the Maasai legend *The Orphan Boy*.

Extending the Theme

• Create a story, as a class or individually, about a boy or girl who wished upon a star and had his or her wish come true.

• Have your class write and illustrate a book titled *Celestial Legends Around the World* by having each student collect a legend from a different country. The legend should focus on the relationship between human and celestial bodies within a cultural or historical setting.

• • • • • • • • • • • • • • •

| Activity 2 | Pictures in the Sky |

Introduction

Have you ever seen a whale, a lion, or a swan in the sky? They are there, just waiting to be seen, when the stars come out, and the sky turns into an enormous picture book. These pictures are created by the stars themselves and finding them is an activity to be shared by young and old from anywhere in the world.

Outcomes

1. To recognize the stars and specific constellations that can be seen in the middle and northern United States

2. To encourage students to become knowledgeable in the identification of specific stars

Materials

• "Pictures in the Sky" worksheet

• suggested reference: *Find the Constellations* by H. A. Rey (Houghton Mifflin, 1988)

Procedure

Using illustrations and reference guides, discuss how stars form constellations. Encourage students to become familiar with several of the constellations and what they look like in the sky. Use the "Pictures in the Sky" worksheet to help reinforce the outlines of these specific constellations. Assign an evening "star watch" to have students attempt to locate the constellations they have been studying.

Extending the Theme

• Draw your own pictures in the sky. Plot stars on a piece of paper and have classmates connect the stars to make a picture.

• Write a new version of the old poem "Twinkle, Twinkle, Little Star."

Name: _____ Date: _____

The Old Man and the Orphan Boy

Setting

Problem

Event

Event

Event

Resolution

Question: The old man in the legend *The Orphan Boy* was very curious about Kileken's secret, and his curiosity left him a lonely man. Have you, like the old man, ever been too curious for your own good? When?

Response: _____

_____

_____

_____

Wishing Upon a Star

List 5 wishes you would make.

1.

2.

3.

4.

5.

Question: How would these five wishes change your life?

Response: _____

_____

_____

_____

_____

Procedure

1. Begin the activity by having the class identify on a physical map or globe the major deserts of the world. Using reference materials and illustrations, discuss how the world's deserts are similar and yet different. The "What Makes a Desert?" worksheet will prove helpful in leading students into such a discussion.

2. Once the class has a general knowledge about how deserts are formed, have each student select a specific world desert to investigate. Have students use the "Desert Detective" worksheet to gather information. When they have collected their data, have them write an illustrated description of their findings, using their worksheets as guides. Collect illustrated descriptions and create a class book titled *Deserts of the World*.

Extending the Theme

- Design a "Deserts of the World" travel brochure.

- Research the diverse plant, animal, and human sounds of specific deserts. Record them on tape or video cassette and have students from other classes identify the many diverse "sounds of the deserts."

• • • • • • • • • • • • • •

| *Activity 2* | **Exploring Desert Cultures Through Archaeology** |

Introduction

The dry desert has preserved, better than any other environment, the artifacts of our human evolution. From the desert dwellings of North America to the ancient ruins of Africa, archaeologists around the world have gathered significant data linking the world's cultural past and present. Their findings consistently communicate a universal cultural heritage rich in resourcefulness and diversity. From the ruins of ancient desert civilizations, students can learn how the technology, economy, government, and rituals of these ancient peoples have provided us with an understanding of our own cultural heritage.

This activity will explore the social and cultural relationships between the desert peoples of the world. Using archaeological data and methods, students will investigate cultural adaptation in relation to environmental change around the world.

Outcomes

1. To demonstrate and utilize archaeological methods in the study of desert cultures

2. To research and critically analyze cultural adaptation in relation to enviromental change

Materials

- reference materials for specific desert cultures throughout the world
- maps
- "Desert Culture Data Sheet" worksheet
- "Digging into a Desert Culture" worksheet
- dirt
- cardboard boxes
- trowels
- rulers
- measuring scales
- string
- masking tape
- scissors

Procedure

1. Using reference materials, introduce students to several desert cultures in varying regions of the world. (Refer to the Desert Bibliography located in the back of this book). Agree on five cultures you would like to compare as a class. Divide students into five cooperative groups. Assign each group a desert culture to investigate. Have them use the worksheet titled "Desert Culture Data Sheet" to collect information about their culture.

2. When students have completed gathering information, they should work in their groups to design, create, and collect artifacts that reflect the lifestyle of the culture they investigated. You will have to help them locate the necessary materials they will need to make their artifacts (clay, feathers, cardboard, etc.).

3. Once the students have completed their artifacts, they should begin designing their "culture box." Fill a cardboard or plastic storage box with dirt. Have students bury their artifacts in the dirt. After the artifacts are buried, use string and masking tape to form a grid on top of the dirt. Label the grid.

4. Prepare students for "Dig Day" by setting up five archaeological sites in the classroom or on the playground. Each site should include a culture box, scale, ruler, trowel, pencil, and enough "Digging into a Desert Culture" worksheets for each child at the archaeological site. You might want to get a parent volunteer to act as a leader for each site.

5. On "Dig Day," students should go to their assigned archaeological site. Arrange sites and students beforehand so that they do not excavate the culture they researched. Each group should have an order of rotation for excavation, measuring, and weighing. Once the artifact has been measured or weighed by the appropriate student, all members of the site record the information on their "Digging into a Desert Culture" worksheet. The dig continues until all grid areas have been excavated.

6. After the dig has been completed, students should meet in their original cooperative groups and analyze the artifacts they have found. This analysis should lead to identification of the excavated culture. When all groups have identified the cultures they excavated, have the class come together and discuss the specific artifacts that helped them to identify their desert cultures. Discuss how specific desert environments influence local lifestyle and compare how these lifestyles are similar and different. Reinforce the importance of the archaeological method as a tool in studying world environments and cultures.

Extending the Theme

- Write a rebus story using illustrations of the artifacts found in a specific desert culture.
- Plan a "People of the Desert" day. Traditional food, dress, and music from diverse desert cultures can be shared and enjoyed by students and their parents.

Name: _____ Date: _____

What Makes a Desert?

List the diverse characteristics of the world's deserts.

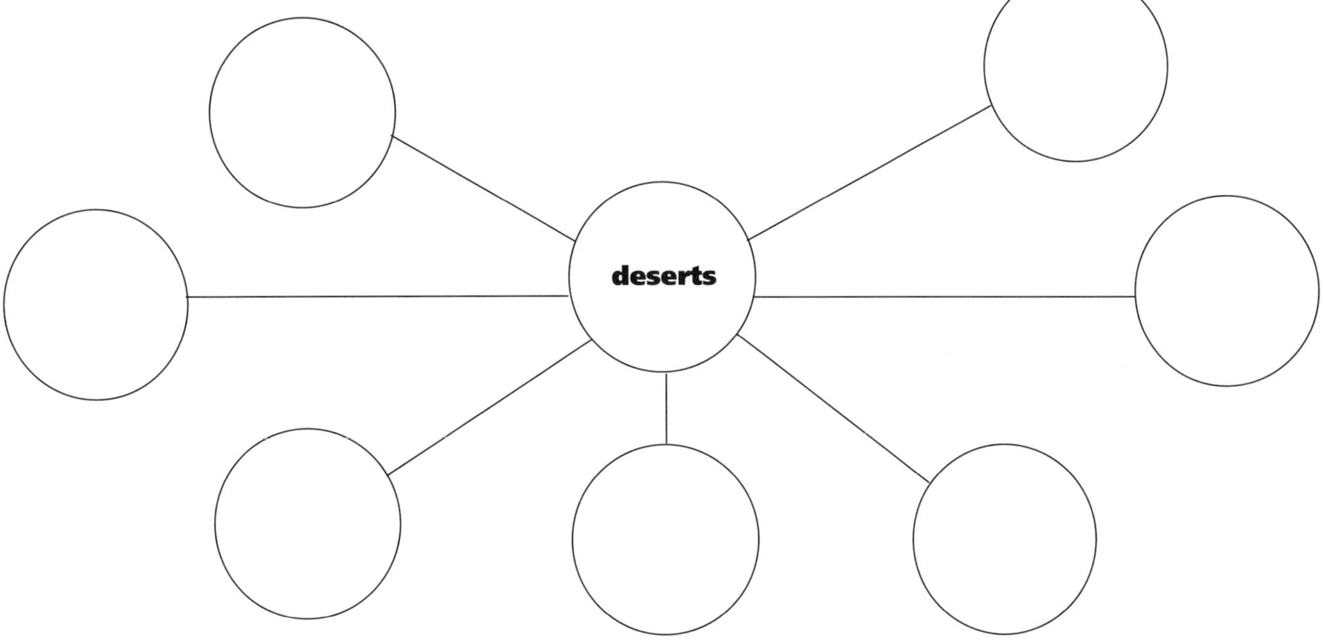

deserts

Question: What characteristics do deserts of the world have in common?

Response: _____

_____

_____

_____

_____

Question: How do deserts of the world differ?

Response: _____

_____

_____

_____

_____

Name: _____   **Date:** _____

Desert Detective

What is the name of your desert?

Where is it located?

How was it formed?

What is the climate like throughout the year?

Describe several plants and how they survive the environment of the desert.

Identify several animals and how they have adapted to the desert environment.

What people live in your desert, and how is their lifestyle influenced by their environment?

Name: _____ **Date:** _____

Desert Culture Data Sheet

Name of People

Geography

Plants

Animals

Economy

Government

Traditions

Beliefs/Religions

Name: _____   Date: _____

Digging into a Desert Culture

Illustration	Artifact Description	Weight	Grid	Centimeters

Introduction

The saguaro, a cactus found only in the Sonoran Desert of southern Arizona and northern Mexico, begins its life with the falling of tiny black saguaro seeds. As it grows, it becomes the home of many different animals who use its fruit to provide food and its flesh to provide shelter.

Students will enjoy the story of the saguaro—a story about a desert, a giant cactus, and the many animals that call it home.

Reading Activity

Cactus Hotel

by Brenda Z. Guiberson (Henry Holt & Company, 1991)

Questions

1. Where is the saguaro cactus found?
2. What is the life cycle of the saguaro cactus?
3. How do animals treat the saguaro cactus like a hotel?
4. How is the fruit of the saguaro cactus used by resident animals?
5. What would happen to the creatures of the desert if the saguaro cactus became endangered?

Outcomes

1. To appreciate the role the saguaro plays in the Sonoran Desert of southern Arizona and northern Mexico
2. To research and analyze relationships between the saguaro and the human and animal populations it supports

Materials

- "Life Cycle of a Saguaro Cactus" worksheet
- pencil

Discussion

From its birth to its death, many animals depend on the saguaro cactus for their survival in the Sonoran desert. Have students discuss the life cycle of the saguaro cactus and the animals it supports. Use the "Life Cycle of a Saguaro Cactus" worksheet to help students plot the relationship between the saguaro's age and the animal life it sustains.

Interdisciplinary Activities

| Activity 1 | **Residents of the Cactus Hotel** |

Introduction

Cactus Hotel by Brenda Guiberson encourages children to explore the dynamics of a desert environment by using the saguaro cactus as the story's main character. As students read about the saguaro, they will become curious about the creatures who reside at the Cactus Hotel. Who are they? Why do they come and why do they leave?

This activity will allow students to create their own stories about the animals who reside at the Cactus Hotel. Using the literary technique of personification, they will provide the animals of the Cactus Hotel with human characteristics, problems, and resolutions. Students should gain from this experience the realization that human and animal needs are very similar in the quest for survival.

Outcomes

1. To gain insight into the dynamic relationships between human and animal populations in the quest for survival

2. To use the literary technique of personification to express, in written form, the problems and resolutions of those animals who reside in the Cactus Hotel

Materials

- reference books about desert animals (see Desert Bibliography)
- "Residents of the Cactus Hotel" worksheet
- composition paper
- drawing paper
- crayons
- markers
- pencils

Procedure

1. Prepare students to write by reviewing some of the animals discussed in the book *Cactus Hotel*. Encourage students to choose three or four animals they wish to study. Divide the class into cooperative groups and assign one animal for each group to research. Provide students with the necessary reference materials to investigate the habitat and lifestyle of their assigned animal.

2. When the cooperative groups have completed their investigation, ask them to think about how the animals they researched have problems similar to the problems people encounter in life. Have them make a list of these similarities.

3. Ask students to think about revising *Cactus Hotel* so the main character is an animal who resides in the hotel, has human-like qualities and a humanlike problem. How would this animal solve the problem and what would be the resolution? Have students create an outline for their story by using the "Residents of the Cactus Hotel" worksheet.

4. When students have completed the outline, they are ready to write and illustrate their stories by elaborating on the details provided by the outline. Students should enjoy sharing their finished stories with each other. They might want to create a booklet titled *Adventures in the Cactus Hotel*.

Extending the Theme

- Have students work in cooperative groups to create skits relative to a Cactus Hotel theme. They can use the stories generated from the "Residents of the Cactus Hotel" worksheet to guide them.

- Design crossword puzzles from the vocabulary introduced while working on the Residents of the Cactus Hotel theme

• • • • • • • • • • • • • •

Activity 2   People of the Saguaro

Introduction

The Papago Indians of the Sonoran desert have depended on the flesh and fruit of the saguaro cactus for centuries. They have used its flesh to construct their houses and its fruit to make a variety of jams, syrups, and wines. The saguaro played such an important role in the lifestyle of the Papago that they began their calendar year with the arrival of its fruit.

The Papago Indians provide students with an wonderful example of the effects local environments have on human populations and visa versa. They will enjoy looking into the world of the Papago, and discovering the what, where, when, and how of their culture.

Outcomes

1. To provide students with an appreciation and respect for the culture of the Papago Indians.

2. To afford students an opportunity to research the relationship between culture and environment

Materials

- reference materials relevant to the Papago Indians (See Desert Bibliography)
- "People of the Saguaro" worksheet

Procedure

Introduce students to the Papago through selected reference materials. Discuss the importance of Papago culture in relationship to their local environment. Use the "People of the Saguaro" worksheet to help students understand the how, when, where, and why of the Papago's reliance on this very special cactus.

Extending the Theme

- Go "Cactus Crazy." Do an investigation on all types of cactuses all around the world. What do they have in common? How do they differ?

- Design a desert mural depicting four or five of the world's most famous deserts.

Name: _____   **Date:** _____

Life Cycle of a Saguaro Tree

Record the life cycle of a saguaro tree.

Birth
```
                          ┌──────────┐
                          │          │
                          └──────────┘
                               │
                          10 │ years
┌──────┐      ┌──────┐    ┌──────────┐    ┌──────┐      ┌──────┐
│      │──────│      │────│          │────│      │──────│      │
└──────┘      └──────┘    └──────────┘    └──────┘      └──────┘
                               │
                          50 │ years
┌──────┐      ┌──────┐    ┌──────────┐    ┌──────┐      ┌──────┐
│      │──────│      │────│          │────│      │──────│      │
└──────┘      └──────┘    └──────────┘    └──────┘      └──────┘
                               │
                          60 │ years
┌──────┐      ┌──────┐    ┌──────────┐    ┌──────┐      ┌──────┐
│      │──────│      │────│          │────│      │──────│      │
└──────┘      └──────┘    └──────────┘    └──────┘      └──────┘
                               │
                         150 │ years
┌──────┐      ┌──────┐    ┌──────────┐    ┌──────┐      ┌──────┐
│      │──────│      │────│          │────│      │──────│      │
└──────┘      └──────┘    └──────────┘    └──────┘      └──────┘
                               │
                         200 │ years
┌──────┐      ┌──────┐    ┌──────────┐    ┌──────┐      ┌──────┐
│      │──────│      │────│          │────│      │──────│      │
└──────┘      └──────┘    └──────────┘    └──────┘      └──────┘
```

Question: The life cycle of the saguaro is influenced by its age. How is your life cycle influenced by your age?

Response: _____

_____

_____

_____

Name: _____ Date: _____

Residents of the Cactus Hotel

Setting:

Main Characters:

Problem:

Event:

Resolution:

Name: _____ Date: _____

People of the Saguaro

Who are the people of the saguaro?

Where do they live?

How do they depend on the saguaro?

When do they use the saguaro?

What do they do with the flesh and fruit of the saguaro?

Why is the saguaro so important to them?

Like the people of the saguaro, what plants do you depend on in your daily life?

41

Introduction

The Mojave desert, a sun-baked land of dramatic beauty, is an ever-changing environment. Its endless stretches of dry, hot land give way to soothing rolling hills. Tumbleweeds dot its landscape, being tossed by the desert's wind. Long-eared jack rabbits, darting lizards, and creeping tortoises find their homes in the desert's shelter.

There are also traces of human occupation. Ghost towns, once alive with miners who sought their fame and fortune, now lie abandoned in the desert's valleys. The dreams of gold and silver lie buried in the crumbling walls they left behind.

Seasonal patterns, along with newly created designs of shape and color, produce many images of the mesmerizing beauty found in the landscape of the Mojave. This theme will explore desert images by focusing on the desert world of the Mojave.

Reading Activity

Mojave

by Diane Siebert (Thomas Y. Crowell, 1988)

Questions

1. Who is the main character of *Mojave*?
2. How does the author describe Mojave's face?
3. How do the seasons influence Mojave's appearance?
4. What does the Mojave hold "deep inside" itself?
5. Why does the author use lyrical prose to describe the Mojave?

Outcomes

1. To explore the environmental dynamics of the Mojave desert
2. To create literary images of desert environments

Materials

- "Desert Images" worksheet
- pencil

Discussion

Diane Siebert uses lyrical prose to create images of the Mojave desert. Ask students to give examples of how Siebert's writing style creates specific "images" of the land, animals, plants, and people native to the Mojave desert. Examples might include: "sweeping face of me," "sting of sand and dust," and "silvery mirages dance." Use the "Desert Images" worksheet to help students record their responses.

Interdisciplinary Activities

Activity 1 Desert Quilt

Introduction

Mountain peaks covered with snow, blossoms of the prickly pear cactus, and autumn breezes are all desert images described by the author of *Mojave*. The seasonal creation of these images give life to a desert world.

This activity will focus on students' collections of desert images—their describing, illustrating, and displaying of the images as a desert quilt.

Outcomes

1. To collect facts about the Mojave desert and put them into statement sentences
2. To illustrate a statement sentence describing the Mojave desert

Materials

- reference materials about the geography, animals, plants, and people of the Mojave desert
- drawing paper
- markers
- crayons
- construction paper
- oaktag
- "Desert Quilt" worksheet
- "Desert Images" worksheet

Procedure

1. Using reference materials, have the class generate a chart of facts that describe the Mojave desert. The "Desert Images" worksheet can be used to help structure this activity.

2. When the chart is completed, have each student select one desert fact and write three statement sentences describing that fact. After they have written their statement sentences, they should illustrate the fact they chose to describe. The "Desert Quilt" worksheet can act as a preliminary draft or a completed assignment.

3. Once students have completed the "Desert Quilt" worksheet, they can begin planning their desert quilt. Students should decide between using the worksheet as a draft or as a completed assignment. When using the worksheet as a draft, provide students with drawing paper, crayons, markers, and so on, to complete their final copies. Once the final copies are finished, they can frame their illustrations using construction paper. A desert quilt should be designed from the framed illustrations. Students are then ready to attach their illustrations to a background of oaktag by gluing or taping them. Desert quilts make wonderful projects to display in the classroom or hallway.

Extending the Theme

- Using index cards, have each student write five facts and five opinions about the Mojave desert. Collect the cards and divide the class into two groups. Develop a game where each group takes turns guessing if the sentence on the index card is an opinion or a fact. Each correct answer is worth one point. The group with the most correct answers wins the game.

- Ballads are wonderful sources for understanding the cultural values of specific groups of people. Research how ballads were used by the miners of the Mojave. What can be learned from ballads about the miner's lifestyle?

. . . .

Activity 2   Desert Poetry

Introduction

The sensory images of the desert provides wonderful material for writing poetry. Imagine touching the hooves of bighorn sheep, hearing the cry of a raven's voice, or touching the spines of a prickly cactus plant. All of these images stimulate children to think about the sensory world around them. This activity will encourage students to write poetry by using sensory images specific to the Mojave desert.

Outcomes

1. To create a poem using the sensory images of the Mojave desert
2. To appreciate the use of our senses in the exploration of world environments

Materials

- "Mojave Desert" worksheet

Procedure

1. Review the five senses and how they are important to writers and poets. What sensory images were created by Siebert in her description of the Mojave desert? How can these images be useful in the writing of a poem?

2. Introduce the "Mojave Desert" worksheet and have each student write a sensory image for each letter in the words Mojave Desert. Students might enjoy reading their poems to the class.

Extending the Theme

- Using index cards, have students design and illustrate postcards with desert scenes. Laminate them and send them to friends.

- Write a spooky story that takes place in a desert setting.

Name: _____ Date: _____

Desert Images

Land	People	Animals	Plants

Name: _____ **Date:** _____

Desert Quilt

Illustration

Statement:

Statement:

Statement:

Mojave Desert Poem

M

O

J

A

V

E

D

E

S

E

R

T

Introduction

It is early morning and the sun is rising. A new day has begun on the seashore, and as the tide goes out, many creatures living on the shore begin their search for shelter from the rising sun. Barrie Watts records the events of many of these sea creatures as they make their way from the early morning sun to the darkness of the night. It is a story of rising and falling tides, camouflage, migration, and most of all, a quest for survival.

Reading Activity

Twenty-four Hours on a Seashore

by Barrie Watts (Franklin Watts, 1990)

Questions

1. How do the tides influence the daily activities of the creatures living on a rocky seashore?
2. What kinds of plants provide a food supply for seashore creatures?
3. How does camouflage protect seashore creatures?
4. How are creatures of the seashore dependent on each other?
5. What would be your favorite time of day or night on the seashore and why?

Outcomes

1. To investigate and explore a rocky seashore habitat during a period of twenty-four hours
2. To have students describe and compare their habitat with that of a rocky seashore

Materials

- "Twenty-four Hours on a Seashore" worksheet
- paper
- colored pencils
- pencil
- crayons
- watercolors

Discussion

Barrie Watts describes a twenty-four hour period on a rocky seashore. He breaks the book up into four parts: 1) early morning, 2) daytime, 3) evening, and 4) night. During each part of the day, he tells how the creatures of the seashore use their natural surroundings to help them in their daily search for food and shelter.

Ask students to chart the daily activities of the seashore by using the timeline found on the "Twenty-four Hours on a Seashore" worksheet. Once students have completed their timeline, they can illustrate what they think would be their favorite time of day or night on a seashore.

Interdisciplinary Activities

Activity 1   Dynamics of a Rocky Seashore Food Chain

Introduction

Animals feeding on each other make up a food chain. Each animal depends on a part of the food chain for survival. If one part of that chain dies, it endangers the entire chain. Sea urchins, for example, feed on mussels while mussels feed on microscopic water life found in plankton. Plankton is carried in the oceans' upper layers and is a major source of food for many creatures of the sea. Polluted water is threatening the nourishment of growing plankton which could possibly have dangerous effects on the seashore food chain.

The purpose of this activity is to encourage students to explore the dynamics of a seashore food chain and the dangers that might inhibit the seashore's survival.

Outcomes

1. To develop a flow chart that reflects a seashore food chain
2. To investigate the dangers facing seashore food chains

Materials

- reference materials specific to seashore food chains (See Seashore bibliography)
- "Dynamics of a Seashore Food Chain" worksheet

Procedure

1. Define the term food chain and discuss how it plays a dynamic role in the daily survival of a seashore environment. Provide examples of how the food chain works by using specific references.

2. Allow students to break up into small groups and develop a flow chart that reflects the dynamics of a seashore food chain. Have them use the "Dynamics of a Seashore Food Chain" worksheet to assist them.

3. When all groups have completed the assignment, ask a representative from each group to share their food chains with the class. Encourage students to discuss the different food chains in different types of seashores.

Extending the Theme

- Create a shoe box diorama of a seashore food chain.
- Write a comparison of a rocky versus a sandy seashore food chain.

•••••••••••••••

Activity 2   Twenty-four Hours in a Habitat

Introduction

Many things happen in a habitat over a twenty-four hour period. Barrie Watts recorded the activities that one might expect to find in a seashore habitat. There are many other habitats, however, and each has its specific wildlife.

Since habitats vary, it might prove interesting to ask your students to record activities that take place in their own habitat over a twenty-four hour period. Their findings can be compared to the activities described by Watts.

Outcomes

1. To keep a record of a specific habitat over a time period of twenty-four hours
2. To compare and contrast the recorded habitat with the seashore habitat described by Watts

Materials

- "Twenty-four Hours in a Habitat" worksheet

Procedure

1. Define the term habitat. What type of activities would students expect to observe during the early morning, daytime, evening, and nighttime in local habitats? Create a list of creatures that might be found and the activities they would be engaged in during the twenty-four hour period.

2. Using the "Twenty-four Hours in a Habitat" worksheet, ask students to document a local habitat by recording the time and activities of various creatures over a twenty-four hour period. As they document information, ask them to compare their observations with those recorded by Barrie Watts.

3. Compare completed observations as a class.

Extending the Theme

- Create a watercolor painting of a local habitat.
- Write a poem describing a seashore over a period of twenty-four hours.

Twenty-four Hours on a Seashore

Using the timeline below, chart the various activities taking place on a seashore during a twenty-four hour period.

early morning	**daytime**	**evening**	**night**

Illustrate your favorite time of day or night on a seashore.

Name: _____ **Date:** _____

Dynamics of a Seashore Food Chain

Show how sea creatures depend on each other by completing the flow chart below.

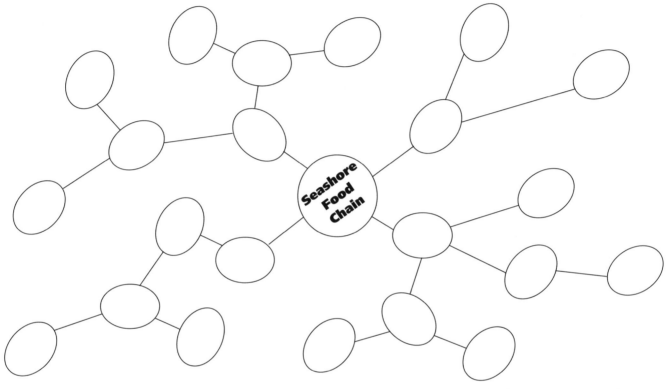

Create a similar flow chart showing how people depend on each other within your community.

Name: _____ **Date:** _____

Twenty-four Hours in a Habitat

Observe and document your natural habitat over a twenty-four hour period. Record your findings and compare them to the seashore habitat described by Watts.

Time	Finding	Comparisons

Images of a Seashore

Introduction

A little boy who had never seen the sea asks his mother "What is the seashore like?" His mother smiles and replies "Let's pretend..." From those few words, Charlotte Zolotow takes her readers on an imaginary visit to a seashore. Using sensory images, she describes mother and son sharing the simple beauty of a beach: the breaking sun, the rising and falling song of the waves, and the evening air from the top of a protruding sand dune.

As the crashing of the waves lull the little boy to sleep, Zolotow's sensitive text, along with Wendell Minor's striking pictures, allow the reader to experience the sensory pleasures of a perfect day at the seashore.

Reading Activity

The Seashore Book

by Charlotte Zolotow (HarperCollins, 1992)

Questions

1. How does the author describe early morning at the seashore?
2. What activities did mother and son share while at the sea?
3. What creatures of the sea were described by the author?
4. How did the author use sensory images to communicate the beauty and pleasures of a day by the sea?
5. How can you relate the images of the seashore to your daily life?

Outcomes

1. To experience a day at the seashore through a sensory description of its beauty
2. To apply the sensory images of the seashore to the observation of student's local environment
3. To develop oral and written communication skills by using sensory images to describe local environments

Materials

- "A Day at the Seashore" worksheet
- pencil

Discussion

Learning to describe our natural surroundings through the use of sensory images is an important tool for effective oral and written communication. Using Zolotow's sensory images and Minor's striking illustrations, ask students to record the sensory words and visions that gave life and meaning to a day at the seashore. The "A Day at the Seashore" worksheet will help guide students through this activity.

You might want to extend this lesson by having your class apply the words and images created by Zolotow and Minor to a special place located within their own environment.

Interdisciplinary Activities

Activity 1 — Exploring the Environment Through Your Senses

Introduction

It is not very often that we get the opportunity to stop working or playing and just listen, observe, smell, or touch an article or object. Such an experience requires us to put our daily routines on hold and to focus our attention on a feature of our environment which usually goes unnoticed in everyday life.

Focusing attention on one aspect of the environment not only takes us away from daily activities, it demands sharp sensory skills. Skills of observation, smelling, tasting, touching, and listening are crucial to understanding any object found in our environment.

This activity will require children to choose a previously unknown feature of their local environment and to use their sensory skills to record its characteristics.

From *Discovering World Cultures Through Literature* published by GoodYearBooks. Copyright © 1995 Gerry Edwards.

Outcomes

1. To investigate an object found in the environment through the use of sensory skills
2. To identify objects found in the environment through a sensory description of its characteristics

Materials

- magnifying glasses
- "Exploring the Environment Through Your Senses" worksheet
- pencils

Procedure

1. Take the class out on the playground or a surrounding area where they will find plants and animals for their investigations. Have them take along the "Exploring the Environment Through Your Senses" worksheet as well as magnifying glasses and pencils.

2. Allow them to walk around and select an object they want to study. Give them a specific amount of time to identify their object and to record 20 of its characteristics.

3. Return to the classroom and ask students to describe several of their object's characteristics by using words that appeal to the senses. Encourage students to identify the various objects studied through sensory descriptions provided by the investigator.

Extending the Theme

- Put students in charge of creating a sixth sense. Ask them what it would be, and how would they use it in their everyday lives.

- Design a postcard of an imaginary visit to a seashore.

• • • • • • • • • • • • • •

Activity 2   Creating a Sense of Place

Introduction

We frequently use words that appeal to the senses to describe the special places we have visited or would like to visit. Activating the senses allows both the writer/reader or the speaker/listener to communicate through the common bond of shared sensory images.

This activity will encourage students to appreciate the usefulness of sensory images in the processes of both written and oral communication.

Outcomes

1. To use sensory language within a written format, to create a "sense" of a favorite place.
2. To orally communicate a "sense of place" to a friend or classmate.

Materials

- reference materials
- illustrations
- "Creating a Sense of Place" worksheet

Procedure

1. Have each student choose a favorite place that they would like to describe for their classmates. It can be a place they have visited or one they became familiar with through other sources (TV, friends, photographs, literature, etc.). Ask each student to visit each place by gathering reference materials that will provide them with the necessary data to complete the assignment.

2. Allow students to use the "Creating a Sense of Place" worksheet to write down their sensory descriptions of the characteristics attributed to their place.

3. Individually or cooperatively, ask students to use their written descriptions to orally communicate a sense of their place to a friend or classmate.

Extending the Theme

- Write a narrative essay describing a pretend visit to a special place.

- Create a collage using various natural materials you might find by a seashore.

A Day at the Seashore

Charlotte Zolotow uses sensory images to describe a visit to the
seashore. How did she use sensory images to describe the following
seashore characteristics?

Sunrise

Water

Sand

Gulls

Waves

Sandpipers

Sailboat

Airplane

Fishing Pier

Evening Air

Top of a Dune

Lighthouse

Rising Evening Tide

Name: _____   Date: _____

Exploring the Environment Through Your Senses

Observe one article in your natural environment. List twenty-five characteristics of the observed article. Have classmates identify the article based on your observations.

Article:

Characteristics:

Name: _____ **Date:** _____

Creating a Sense of Place

Create sensory images to create your favorite place.

Introduction

The elements of the seashore, its rising and falling tides, sunrises and sunsets, and bountiful plant and animal life provide a source of inspiration as well as survival for many peoples of the world. Although the types of seashores and the ways each was formed vary, they are all alike in that they exhibit environments where land and water meet to create specific habitats for local and migratory animal and human populations.

Lynn Stone, author of *Seashores*, explores the types of seashores and how they were formed along the east and west coasts of the United States and Canada. The plants and animals of specific seashore habitats are discussed, along with the need to protect seashore environments through conservation.

Reading Activity

Seashores

by Lynn M. Stone (Rourke Enterprises, Incorporated, 1989)

Questions

1. What different types of seashores can be found in the United States and Canada?
2. What geological events influenced the formation of seashores along the Pacific and Atlantic coasts of North America?
3. How do salt marshes fit into the ecosystem of seashores located on the Atlantic coast?
4. Where would you find an estuary?
5. How can conservationists help to protect seashore environments?

Outcomes

1. To identify and define geographical terms that refer to seashore environments
2. To investigate the different types of seashores and how they were formed
3. To explore plant and animal life of various seashore habitats

Materials

- "Seashore Vocabulary" worksheet
- pencil
- words from the student-generated word bank

Discussion

Lynn Stone provides students with a great deal of information concerning the different types of seashore habitats along the coasts of the United States and Canada.

Encourage students to generate a word bank by recalling terms that are specific to seashore environments. Divide the class into groups of two and have each group look up two to three vocabulary words from the word bank. Share definitions and discuss how each applies to the understanding of seashore habitats.

Using the "Seashore Vocabulary" worksheet, ask students to write a sentence for each of the vocabulary words listed in the word bank.

Interdisciplinary Activities

Activity 1   Seashore Animals

Introduction

Animals living in seashore habitats are broken down into two primary categories, those with backbones (vertebrates), and those without backbones (invertebrates). Animals categorized as invertebrates include coelenterates, echinoderms, annelids, mollusks, and arthropods. Animals categorized as vertebrates include fish, amphibians, reptiles, birds, and mammals.

This activity will require students to identify animals from each group and to address, in writing, how people living near or on the seashore depend on these animals for their daily existence.

Outcomes

1. To identify and classify specific seashore animals
2. To write an essay concerning the importance of seashore animals to the subsistence of surrounding human populations

Materials

- reference materials (see Seashore bibliography)
- "Seashore Animals" worksheet

Procedure

1. Introduce the terms vertebrate and invertebrate. Using the "Seashore Animals" worksheet, encourage students to identify and classify specific animals by recording them in the appropriate category. Distribute any reference materials students might need to accomplish the assignment.

2. Culminate this activity with class discussion and individual writing responses to the question: How do people from the many different parts of the world depend on seashore animals for their daily subsistence?

Extending the Theme

- Working in groups, ask students to develop a crossword puzzle using geographical terms relating to seashore environments.
- Have students pretend they are a seashore animal, and write an autobiography.

• • • • • • • • • • • • • •

Activity 2 Seashore Sites: United States and Canada

Introduction

There are many outstanding seashore sites that stretch the coasts of the United States and Canada. Many of these sites have been designated as National Seashores or Parks and are visited by people from all over the world.

This activity will inspire students to examine several National Seashores and to plot their locations on a map.

Outcomes

1. To identify and plot several National Seashores on a map
2. To examine the diverse habitats of several National Seashores or Parks

Materials

- encyclopedias
- travel brochures
- photographs of National Seashores
- "Seashore Sites: United States and Canada" worksheet

Procedure

1. Using reference materials and the "Seashore Sites: United States and Canada" worksheet, identify and plot specific seashore sites.

2. Ask students to compare and contrast the diverse National Seashores and Parks. How are geographical features and animal and plant life populations similar and different between the east and west coasts? How are these seashores used as resort areas, and what are the dangers imposed on them by the resort industry? What are the conservational concerns for each site, and what agencies are helping to protect the survival of these National Seashores and Parks?

3. You might want to culminate this activity by asking students to choose a National Seashore they would like to visit and to explain the reasons behind their choice.

Extending the Theme

- Design a plan or proposal for saving a National Seashore or Park located in the United States or Canada.
- Plan a trip from Maine to Florida and write an itinerary for visiting several National Seashores or Parks along the way. Include the names and locations of where you would stay, the places and sites you would visit while at each National Seashore or Park, and the reasons you selected each site.

Name: _____ **Date:** _____

Seashore Vocabulary

estuary   plankton
glaciation   sea stack
habitat   wrack
intertidal   zonation

Use each of the above words in a sentence.

1.

2.

3.

4.

5.

6.

7.

8.

Seashore Animals

How do people living near or on a seashore depend on the animals below for their subsistence?

Invertebrate	Vertebrate
coelenterates:	fish:
echinoderms:	amphibians:
annelids:	reptiles:
mollusks:	birds:
arthropods:	mammals:

Name: _____   Date: _____

Seashore Sites: United States and Canada

Plot the following seashore sites on the map below. Write a brief description of each site.

Point Lobos State Reserve: Acadia National Park:

Canaveral National Seashore: Cape Hatteras National Seashore:

Cape Cod National Seashore: Padre Island National Seashore:

Introduction

California's stately Sierra Nevada was formed many millions of years ago when the earth was young. These majestic mountains have seen centuries come and go. They have sheltered animals, big and small, such as the shy pika and the big black bear. They have been home to many different cultures including the Indians who hunted their animals and the cowboys who traveled their vast ranges. Century after century, the Sierra Nevada has witnessed and played a meaningful role in a changing environment and world.

This theme will ask students to take a journey, using their senses of sight, sound, touch, taste, and smell, to explore the mountain range known as the Sierra Nevada.

Reading Activity

Sierra

by Diane Siebert (HarperCollins, 1991)

Questions

1. How were the mountains of the Sierra formed?
2. What animals find shelter in the Sierra?
3. How does the author describe the glaciers of long ago?
4. How does the author personify the Sierra?
5. What will happen to the Sierra as time passes?

Outcomes

1. To explore the ecosystem of the Sierra Nevada through the senses of sight, sound, touch, taste, and smell
2. To relate the life cycle of a mountain range to our own

Materials

- "The World of the Sierra" worksheet
- pencil

Discussion

The author of *Sierra* uses wonderful descriptive phrases to portray the majestic world of the Sierra Nevada. Phrases such as "watchful peaks that pierce the skies," the sequoia's "endless quest for sky," and the coming of the sea which brings "constant winds to conquer me" all create sensory visions of the magnificent beauty found in the Sierra.

Using "The World of the Sierra" worksheet, encourage students to recount phrases that were written by the author to describe specific features of the Sierra Nevada. Have them record their responses on the worksheet. Discuss what phrases they might use to describe the same features and how these phrases would help the reader to visualize the Sierra's ecosystem.

Interdisciplinary Activities

Activity 1   A Sensory Journey to the Sierra

Introduction

Our senses are marvelous tools for exploring the world around us. They allow us to see an eagle in flight, feel an animal's fur, smell a skunk's scent, hear a bird's cry, and taste raindrops.

This activity will stimulate students to create sensory images from the very powerful and beautifully illustrated paintings of Wendell Minor. It is a journey that will provide them with an opportunity to capture the awe-inspiring splendor of a mountain region by using their senses.

Outcomes

1. To create sensory images of a mountain region through the paintings of Wendell Minor
2. To demonstrate the importance of sensory images in the description of environmental settings

Materials

- "A Sensory Journey" worksheet
- Wendell Minor's paintings found in Siebert's book *Sierra*
- "The World of the Sierra" worksheet (optional)

Procedure

1. Review how our senses help us to create images of everyday life within our environmental settings. Ask students to develop sensory images from clue words such as water, sky, animal, plant, and land. You might choose "The World of the Sierra" worksheet to illustrate how descriptive phrases appeal to specific senses.

2. Introduce the paintings of Wendell Minor and discuss how they create sensory images. Students might benefit by a second reading of the book. This time, however, the focus should be on the illustrations rather than the text.

3. Using the "A Sensory Journey" worksheet, have students choose a favorite Wendell Minor picture, illustrate it, and describe the sensory images they can glean from the painting. Students will enjoy sharing their sensory images as a class.

Extending the Theme

- Write a historical fiction story using the Sierra Nevada as a setting.
- Use Wendell Minor's paintings as a springboard to a cumulative class story.

• • • • • • • • • • • • • •

Activity 2   Mountain Relations

Introduction

Siebert personifies the mountains of the grand Sierra by endowing them with the qualities of life: "I've stood, and watching time unfold, have known the age of ice and snow. And what my course of life will be depends on how man cares for me. . . For mountains live and mountains die, As ages pass, so too, will I." The lifelike characteristics created by Siebert allow her readers to relate to the Sierra as another living entity. The identity with nature as a "living" force in our lives generates feelings of empathy and concern for the natural world surrounding us.

This activity will encourage students to compare and contrast the living qualities of nature with their own. It is an activity which promotes a global perspective by asking students to relate to the natural world around them.

Outcomes

1. To compare and contrast the living qualities of people with nature
2. To encourage appreciation of the living qualities shared by people and nature around the world

Materials

- "Mountain Relations" worksheet

Procedure

1. Introduce the literary technique of personification by asking students how Siebert gave humanlike qualities to the mountains of the Sierra. Develop a list of quotes from the book *Sierra* that portray the mountains as living entities.

2. Allow students time to think about how the living qualities of the Sierra relate to their own lives. The "Mountain Relations" worksheet will help guide students in this activity.

3. When the assignment is completed, ask students to share their responses as a class. Discuss the importance of developing a global perspective of world environments that includes people and nature working together to secure the future of both.

Extending the Theme

- Write an epitaph for the Sierra Nevada that would be reflective of a global perspective that is not supportive of people and nature working together.
- Develop a list of assumptions people have about the mountain regions of the world.

The World of the Sierra

Feature: Mountain

Descriptive Phrase

Feature: Glacier

Descriptive Phrase

Feature: Predators

Descriptive Phrase

Feature: Waterfalls

Descriptive Phrase

Feature: Pines

Descriptive Phrase

Feature: Storms

Descriptive Phrase

Feature: Sequoias

Descriptive Phrase

A Sensory Journey

Illustration:

I Can See . . .

I Can Hear . . .

I Can Touch . . .

I Can Smell . . .

I Can Taste . . .

Name: _____ Date: _____

Mountain Relations

Quote:

Response:

Quote:

Response :

Quote:

Response:

Quote:

Response:

Quote:

Response:

The World's Endangered Mountain Animals

Introduction

The landscape of a mountain region supports a variety of wildlife. Grazing elk might be found on a mountain's grassy foothills, while grizzly bears might prefer to stalk the pine forests of higher habitats. The food supplied by dwarf trees and small plants will entice the bighorns of still higher mountain habitats. Many of the animals found in these mountain habitats are endangered. Erosion, compounded by the human activities of logging, mining, farming, ranching, road-building, and hunting, is destroying the homes of many mountain animals.

This theme will focus on the exploration of the world's endangered mountain animals by identifying these animals and investigating the dangers and concerns facing their survival.

Reading Activity

Endangered Mountain Animals

by Dave Taylor (Crabtree Publishing Co., 1992)

Questions

1. What are two ways mountains are created?
2. What animals live on the different levels of a mountain?
3. How is erosion a danger to mountain habitats?
4. What human activities are threatening the habitats of many mountain animals?
5. Why is it important to support the survival of mountain animals around the world?

Outcomes

1. To identify the world's endangered mountain animals
2. To investigate, research, and analyze the concerns and dangers facing the world's endangered mountain animals

Materials

- "Endangered Mountain Animals of the World" worksheet
- reference materials listing animals in danger of becoming extinct
- pencil
- map or globe

Discussion

Endangered mountain animals can be found on all of the earth's continents. The honey bear of Southeast Asia, the bongo of Africa, the Andean flamingo of South America, and the endeared panda of China are all examples of mountain animals facing extinction.

The dangers facing these mountain animals differ depending on the specific mountain habitat. Pandas are considered endangered animals due to poaching (illegal killing), and dying bamboo supplies. The Andean flamingo, on the other hand, faces extinction as a result of polluted lakes, where they traditionally catch most of their food.

Using the "Endangered Mountain Animals of the World" worksheet, have students identify specific animal populations in risk of becoming extinct, where these animals are located, and the dangers facing their survival. When students have completed the assignment, have them locate the identified animal populations on a map or globe. Discuss how people can help save the world's endangered mountain animals.

Interdisciplinary Activities

| Activity 1 | Human Dangers to Animals Living in Mountain Habitats |

Introduction

Many of the dangers facing mountain animals are created by human populations. The hunting of animals, legally or illegally, is a legacy in many world cultures. Whether for food, sport, or money, hunting is a social and cultural tradition that resists the forces of change.

Responding to the demands of increasing human populations has led to the farming of lands which were once grazing spots for mountain animals. Again, "farming the land" carries with it a heritage of powerful cultural traditions. These traditions place human need above animal survival.

Logging, mining, and ranching, all human activities produced by the spirit of industrialization, have created cultural beliefs rooted in themes of technological progress through environmental exploitation. The global pollution and staggering changes in the world's mountain habitats is viewed as an unfortunate trade-off for the advancement of civilization.

The following activity will ask students to investigate the dangers facing mountain animals and their habitats because of human intervention.

Outcomes

1. To identify cultural traditions and practices being used by human populations in mountain regions around the world
2. To analyze and evaluate how human traditions and practices are endangering the survival of mountain animals

Materials

- reference books and illustrations about farming, logging, mining, and hunting communities (See Mountain bibliography)
- "Human Dangers to Animal Populations" worksheet

Procedure

1. Introduce how human practices are endangering the survival of many mountain animals by using illustrations and reference materials taken from the bibliography. Have students discuss how the cultural traditions found in hunting, farming, mining, and logging might influence the survival of specific mountain animals. Hunters, for example, practice rituals before and after a hunt. Farming often follows specific seasonal patterns of practice. Occupations such as logging, mining, and ranching all possess bodies of folklore to preserve the identity and purpose of their cultural traditions.

2. Ask each student to investigate one endangered mountain animal. Crucial to the investigation will be inquiry into the human practices that are putting the animal's survival at risk. What are these practices? How do cultural traditions support these practices? How are these practices endangering the survival of the student's chosen mountain animal?

3. It is also important for students to develop a resolution which supports a plan of action to save their specific mountain animal. Use the "Human Dangers to Animal Populations" worksheet to help students complete the assignment.

4. When the class has finished the assignment, have them compare and contrast how their animals are being threatened by the same, different, or similar human practices.

Extending the Theme

- Write a fable where the main character is an endangered mountain animal. What lesson would the fable teach?
- Create a TV commercial that would support the survival of endangered mountain animals.

• • • • • • • • • • • • • •

Activity 2   **Taking a Stand: What Are People Doing to Help Endangered Mountain Animals Around the World?**

Introduction

There are many people trying to save endangered mountain animals. Private agencies such as the Wilderness Society and the Sierra Club are very active in their pursuit to guarantee survival for these animals.

Government policies at both federal and local levels are contributing to the safety of mountain wildlife by legislating hunting restrictions on specific animal populations.

Private citizens are doing their part by becoming knowledgeable about the issues facing endangered animals and supporting the agencies and policies that will benefit endangered mountain species.

Most important, many schoolchildren are becoming globally aware of the delicate balance between people and the environment. Such an awareness will generate an environmental perspective that supports greater respect and concern for the relationship between people and nature.

This activity will require students to learn about the people who are helping to save mountain wildlife around the world. It will also ask them to think about how they can make a difference in the quest for animal survival.

Outcomes

1. To identify private and governmental agencies, policies, and practices that are helping to secure the survival of mountain animals
2. To explore the role students can play in the quest to save mountain wildlife

Materials

- composition paper
- "Taking a Stand: How Are People Helping Endangered Animals?" worksheet
- letter outline worksheet
- recent almanac

Procedure

1. Have the class develop a list of private and government agencies that are actively working to save mountain wildlife. Use the "Taking a Stand: How Are People Helping Endangered Animals?" worksheet as a guide to developing the list.

2. Ask each student to choose an agency and write a letter requesting specifically what that agency is doing to help endangered mountain animals. An almanac might be useful in getting the addresses for these organizations. As students receive the information from the different agencies, have them share it with the class.

3. Culminate the activity by having students write a paper explaining their stand on the preservation of mountain wildlife. It should be based on the information gathered and discussed in class.

Extending the Theme

- Have students write a speech supporting their stand on the issue of endangered mountain animals.
- Stage a classroom debate on the pros and cons of developing policies and practices that will secure survival of mountain wildlife.

Endangered Mountain Animals of the World

Animal:

Location:

Dangers:

Animal:

Location:

Dangers:

Animal:

Location:

Dangers:

Animal:

Location:

Dangers:

Animal:

Location:

Dangers:

Animal:

Location:

Dangers:

Human Dangers to Animal Populations

Human Practice:

Cultural Traditions Supporting Practice

Dangers to Mountain Animal Populations

Human Practice:

Cultural Traditions Supporting Practice

Dangers to Mountain Animal Populations

Human Practice:

Cultural Traditions Supporting Practice

Dangers to Mountain Animal Populations

Human Practice:

Cultural Traditions Supporting Practice

Dangers to Mountain Animal Populations

Name: _____ Date: _____

Taking a Stand: How Are People Helping Endangered Animals?

Agency:

Stand:

Agency:

Stand:

Agency:

Stand:

Agency:

Stand:

Agency:

Stand:

Agency:

Stand

Reading Activity

Appalachia

by Cynthia Rylant (Harcourt Brace Jovanovich, 1991)

Questions

1. How do the good dogs found in Appalachia fit into the Appalachian lifestyle?

2. Why do most people raised in Appalachia choose to stay there for the duration of their lives?

3. Most of the people living in Appalachia are thinkers. How are you like the thinkers of Appalachia?

4. What daily or seasonal activities are specific to Appalachian women?

5. What is a Sunday in Appalachia like?

Introduction

The Appalachian mountains stretch from Quebec, Canada, to central Alabama. The land where the Appalachian mountains pass through Tennessee and West Virginia is often referred to as "Appalachia." Appalachia boasts a lifestyle encompassing good dogs, hard-working coal-miners, and homemade cherry cobbler. Its people are proud churchgoers who find their sense of identity and purpose from the mountains that surround them.

This theme will take students on a journey to visit the people of Appalachia. It is a journey which will inspire students to look at a way of life that is different, yet similar to their own.

Outcomes

1. To investigate and examine the lifestyle of the people who inhabit the area known as Appalachia

2. To have students compare and contrast their lifestyle with that of the Appalachian people

Materials

• "Comparing Two Lifestyles" worksheet
• pencil

Discussion

The lifestyle found in Appalachia might be described as rural or country as opposed to an urban or city lifestyle. The two lifestyles may seem worlds apart in terms of daily habits and cultural practices, but they embrace many of the same values. What are these values, and how do they influence the lifestyles of the people who respect them?

Using the "Comparing Two Lifestyles" worksheet, have students plot the different lifestyle practices one would expect to find in urban versus rural settings. Where the two circles overlap, have students record similar values shared by urban and rural dwellers.

The response question will encourage each child to think about the relationship between cultural practices and beliefs.

Interdisciplinary Activities

| Activity 1 | **Practice What You Preach** |

Introduction

There is an old American saying that advises the wise to "practice what you preach." This saying found its roots in Colonial America and was passed on by many succeeding generations as an effort to encourage people to live their lives according to their values and beliefs. American beliefs and values have not changed significantly since Colonial days. However, American practices in response to those beliefs and values have changes dramatically. This activity will require students to think about what they do in their everyday lives and why they do it.

Outcomes

1. To investigate and analyze the cultural beliefs and practices of Appalachia
2. To have students record their cultural practices and critically evaluate these practices in connection to their cultural beliefs

Materials

- "Practice What You Preach" worksheet

Procedure

1. Begin by asking students what motivates their behaviors or actions. Why do some children obey or disobey their parents and teachers? Why do some children cheat on tests? Why do some people celebrate Thanksgiving? Have the class make a list of different practices carried out daily, seasonally, or throughout a lifetime (marriage, baptism, etc.), by different people. Try to have the students develop categories for the practices listed. Examples might include home, family, friends, school, and playground.

2. Once the list is completed, encourage students to observe that actions are rooted in choice. Discuss different practices on the list and how choice influenced the actual behavior. Go a step further by having students evaluate why they choose a specific behavior. They should be able to see that where their behavior is linked to a choice, their choice is a response to an underlying value or belief. Use the "Practice What You Preach" worksheet to assess the relationship between practices and underlying values. When students have completed the assignment, have them share their thoughts about practicing what they preach.

Extending the Theme

- Explore the traditional customs and practices of a country outside of the United States. Analyze how their customs and practices relate to specific beliefs and values. Compare those values with those found in the United States.

- Research superstitions that have developed in America to warn people of the consequences of not carrying out specific beliefs.

• • • • • • • • • • • • • • •

Activity 2   Coal Miners and Their Folklore

Introduction

The mountains of Appalachia are abundant with coal, and many people living in this region have supported their families for generations by coal mining. The coal miner is first and foremost a "family man," one willing to risk the dangers of a cave-in, explosion, or fire that could spread death throughout the shafts and tunnels of the coal miner's world.

Due to the dangers and risks involved in being a coal miner, many stories, songs, and customs evolved that portrayed the pride, fearlessness, and heroism of a coal miner in the midst of his peril. These stories were told to younger generations and became a form of oral tradition, or folklore, among coal-mining families.

This theme will encourage students to investigate the lifestyle of Appalachia's coal miners through their folklore. They will find the coal-mining stories to be a part of American history rich in the values of pride, hard work, and dedication to family.

Outcomes

1. To gain an understanding and respect for the lifestyle of coal-mining families through their folklore
2. To pursue a historical appreciation for the role played by coal miners in the evolution of American culture

Materials

- reference materials specific to coal miners and their folklore (See Mountain Regions bibliography)
- "Coal Miners Folklore" worksheet

Procedure

1. Introduce folklore as a study which uses oral tradition found in proverbs, legends, ballads, customs, beliefs, and values to analyze and understand a specific group's culture.

2. Lead students into a discussion about the lifestyle of coal-mining communities and how their folklore helps us to understand their culture. Using the above sources (proverbs, legends, ballads, customs, and beliefs), provide examples of how coal miners generate their folklore and why.

3. You might want students to research the following names and events which would help them understand the origins of much of the coal mining folklore: Pat Dolan, Mines of Avondale, Jimmy Kerrigan's confession, Thomas Duffy, Molly Maguires, and Black Thursday. Discuss how these folk heroes or events were crucial to the development of coal mining folklore.

4. Break students up into groups and have them collect one specific source of folklore (proverbs, superstitions, etc.). When they have completed their investigation, have students come together and discuss and record their findings as a class. Use the "Coal Miner's Folklore" worksheet to assist students in recording their data.

Extending the Theme

- Coal miners formed very active and powerful labor unions. Have students investigate the union history of coal miners and create a poster which reflects a cause they would have supported.

- Davy Crockett, a tall, black-haired hunter and trapper from the mountains of Tennessee, became one of America's greatest heroes. Explore the folklore generated by Crockett's life, and why America regarded him as such a hero. Compare Crockett's personal characteristics and deeds with those of the coal miners.

Comparing Two Lifestyles

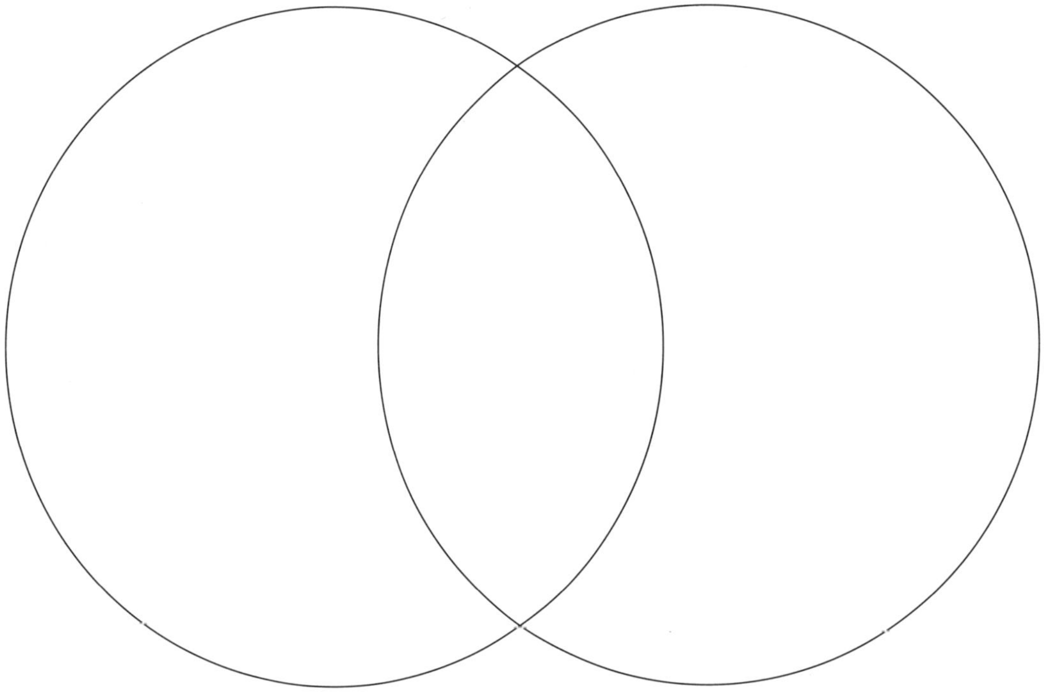

Question: Why do rural and urban populations have different everyday practices but similar cultural values?

Response: _____

_____

_____

_____

_____

Name: _____   Date: _____

Practice What You Preach

Practice:

Value:

Practice:

Value:

Practice:

Value

Practice:

Value:

Practice:

Value:

Coal Miners' Folklore

Proverbs

Superstitions

Legends

Ballads

Customs

Beliefs

Polar Landscapes

Introduction

Polar landscapes are filled with a diverse beauty created by massive regions of ice as well as vast treeless areas known as *tundra*. This is the home of the ringed seal, polar bear, and emperor penguin. It is also the home of the *Inuit,* more frequently referred to as the Eskimo, who subsist on the plant and animal life provided by the polar environment.

This theme will explore the similarities and differences of the two polar landscapes most commonly known as the Arctic and the Antarctic. Students will study the climate of each as well as the land, water, plants, animals, and human life that make polar regions unique and fascinating areas of inquiry.

Reading Activity

Ecology Watch: Polar Lands

by Rodney Aldis (Dillion Press, 1992)

Questions

1. What does the term *poles apart* mean?
2. What are the three types of ice found in a polar region?
3. Who are the "hunters of the wilderness" and what do they hunt?
4. How are penguins dressed for survival?
5. How is the process of adaptation revealed among the animals who live in the world's polar lands?

Outcomes

1. To investigate the climate, land, water, plant, animal, and human populations of the two polar regions known as the Arctic and the Antarctic
2. To gain an appreciation of the Arctic and the Antarctic as frontier environments in need of human respect for survival

Materials

- "Poles Apart" worksheet
- pencil

Discussion

Geographers tend to define polar regions by climate rather than forest-tundra boundaries. The Arctic and Antarctic boundaries are made up of imaginary lines, called *isotherms.* These lines link points on the earth's surface where the average temperature for the warmest month is 50 degrees Farenheit. The climatic boundary in the Arctic tends to follow the northern limits of the forests. The boundary of the Antarctic is out on an open ocean where the cold waters of the Antarctic ocean meet with the warm waters flowing from the tropics. An illustration of how different the two poles look can be found on pages 6 and 7 of the reading selection.

Encourage students to become familiar with the diversity of the two poles by having them do the "Poles Apart" worksheet. Using the illustration provided by Aldis, have students plot the crucial physical features for each pole and develop a map key reflective of those features.

When the class has completed their maps, ask students to think about how the diverse physical features of the two poles influence their appearance and the types of plant, animal, and human life they can support. Have them respond by answering the question on the "Poles Apart" worksheet.

Interdisciplinary Activities

Activity 1   Ice, Ice, and More Ice

Introduction

A polar landscape almost always contains ice. There are three types of ice: landfast ice, pack ice, and icebergs. Each plays a role in supporting the plant, animal, and human life of a polar environment.

Landfast ice, ice joined to the land, begins its bonding with the land in early winter. By midwinter, it has secured its place between the land and the offshore pack ice. During the spring, the pack ice breaks up faster than the landfast ice can melt. This results in the formation of a wide shelf separating the open water from the shore. Arctic polar bears and Eskimos hunt for seals along this annually created ledge.

Pack ice is made from frozen seawater and can be found in both polar oceans. In certain areas, such as the central part of the Arctic Ocean, pack ice remains permanently frozen. In other areas, summer's higher temperatures and ocean currents break up the pack ice, creating floating sheets of ice known as *floes*. These floes often present a hazard for ships sailing to polar lands.

Icebergs are created when glaciers and ice sheets reach the coast and drift with the currents until they melt. On average, they are about the size of a shopping mall. The platforms created by drifting icebergs are used as resting places by some seabirds.

All three major forms of ice are important to the plant, animal, and human populations who depend on them as a necessary resource for their own survival. If the ice was to melt because of greenhouse gases, the increased ocean level would flood urban cities as well as rural farming areas. Therefore, an effort to save our polar landscapes is an effort to save our planet.

Outcomes	**Materials**
1. Equate the three types of ice found in polar landscapes with the plant, animal, and human populations they support 2. Recognize how important ice is to the survival of polar regions	• "Ice, Ice, and More Ice" worksheet

Procedure

1. Introduce the three types of ice found in polar landscapes. State the importance each type has to specific plant, animal, and human populations. The "Ice, Ice, and More Ice" worksheet will help students record information as it is being discussed.

2. Encourage the class to think about how greenhouse gases could influence polar ice masses. Ask students what they think would happen to our planet if polar region ice melted. When the assignment has been completed, have students create a list of ways they can help save polar landscapes.

Extending the Theme

• Develop a word search using vocabulary words that relate to polar regions. Students can exchange completed word searches.

• Write a character sketch for an animal found in a polar landscape. Ask students to take turns sharing their character sketches, while classmates attempt to guess the name of the animal being sketched.

• • • • • • • • • • • • • • •

Activity 2   Hunters of the Ice

Introduction

The indigenous peoples of the Arctic, known as the Inuit, have gathered plants and hunted animals for centuries. They understand the plants, animals, and people of the Arctic comprise a food chain that must be respected in order to be maintained. This respect for nature is reflected in their traditional hunting practices and beliefs.

The Inuit were introduced to new technological practices and foods through European contact. They began to hunt animals solely for the animal's skin or fur. The Inuits sell the skins and furs of the seal, polar bear, and Arctic fox to buy fuel and modern hunting equipment. Although life changed dramatically for the Inuit as a result of European contact, they still remain a hunting culture and continue to rely on the animals of the Arctic for their subsistence.

The Inuit of today are living between two worlds. Traditional hunting beliefs and practices are being challenged by changing technology. Mining and oil drilling are threatening the plant and animal life the Inuit rely on for their survival. Many Inuit are leaving the traditional practices of their ancestors behind and becoming wage earners instead of hunters. They are living in year-round, permanent settlements and establishing households based on the nuclear, instead of the extended, family.

The dynamics of cultural contact has dramatically changed the Inuit populations of the Arctic forever. The Inuit realize, however, that whatever lifestyle they choose, it must be nurtured by a respect for the environment that supports and maintains their existence.

Outcomes

1. Recognize ways the Inuit culture has changed because of contact with people from other parts of the world
2. To better understand that some of these changes are needed for survival

Materials

- "Hunters of the Ice" worksheet

Procedure

1. Introduce the Inuit, their traditional hunting practices, and how those practices were altered as a result of European contact. Draw a chart with two columns. Label one column "Precontact" and the second column "Postcontact." List appropriate beliefs, values, and practices in each column.

2. Using the "Hunters of the Ice" worksheet, have students write an essay discussing how hunting practices of the Inuit have changed in response to European contact. Have them include their feelings about the changes in Inuit lifestyle. Also, have them predict how these changes might influence the Inuit's future. Share the essays as a class.

Extending the Theme

- We all meet people who influence our lives. Describe a friend, relative, or stranger who made a significant change in your life.
- Pretend you are writing an advice column. What advice would you give to the Inuit?

Name: _____ **Date:** _____

Poles Apart

Label the physical features of both poles and create a map key that illustrates those features.

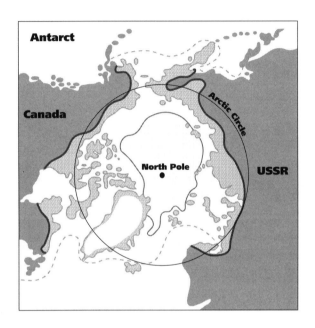

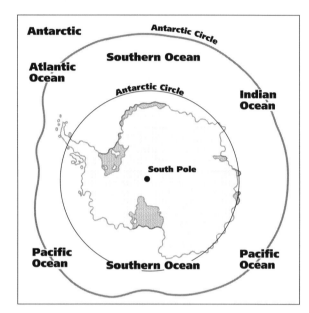

Question: How do the diverse physical features of the two poles influence their appearance and the types of plant, animal, and human life they can support?

Response: _____

_____

_____

_____

_____

Name: _____ Date: _____

Ice, Ice, and More Ice

Ice is a common feature of polar landscapes. There are three types of ice: icebergs, pack ice, and landfast ice. Describe each type and its role in a polar environment.

Icebergs:

Pack Ice:

Landfast Ice:

Question: What would happen to our planet if all the ice of the polar regions melted?

Response: _____

_____

_____

_____

_____

Hunters of the Ice

Essay: Discuss how hunting practices of the Inuit have changed in response to European contact. How do you feel about these changes? How might these changes influence the future of the Inuit?

Oil Spill: Legacy of the Exxon Valdez

Introduction

It was a windless night in the spring of 1989. An oil tanker, the *Exxon Valdez,* hit a reef in the Prince William Sound, located off Alaska's southern coast. Eleven million gallons of crude oil spilled into the sound's pristine waters, eventually killing hundreds of thousands of birds and sea mammals.

Rescue workers made a courageous effort to save endangered animals from their oil-contaminated habitats. However the oil spill, the worst in U.S. history, left in its wake an environmental lesson for everyone. Terry Carr recounts the event by carefully taking us back to the night of the fateful accident, to the heroic and heart-rending rescue scenes. His book gives us a clearer understanding of the political ramifications of this environmental disaster.

Reading Activity

Spill! The Story of the Exxon Valdez

by Terry Carr (Franklin Watts, 1991)

Questions

1. How did the collision of the Exxon Valdez take place?
2. Name some problems encountered by rescue workers after the spill.
3. How were birds and sea mammals specifically affected by the spill?
4. What political ramifications surfaced as a result of the spill?
5. Why did the author write this book?

Outcomes

1. To better understand the causes of the collision of the *Exxon Valdez,* the rescue efforts to save wildlife, and the political ramifications that followed this environmental disaster
2. To research and analyze the controversial issues created by human exploitation of environmental resources

Materials

- "The Pros and Cons of Mixing Oil and Nature" worksheet
- pencil

Discussion

The story of the *Exxon Valdez* was heard around the world. It is a story that asks many questions and teaches many lessons. Ask students to discuss the lessons and questions generated by the oil spill in Alaska.

It is important for students to realize the complexity of the issues surrounding the exploitation of oil in pristine environments. There are many pros and cons concerning the oil industry and its influence on nature as well as Native Alaskans.

Using "The Pros and Cons of Mixing Oil and Nature" worksheet, encourage students to explore the positive and negative factors of economic growth through the oil industry in Alaska. Next ask them to take a position on this issue by responding to the question "Do oil and nature mix?" Your class might enjoy culminating this activity by breaking up into debating teams and arguing their positions.

Interdisciplinary Activities

Activity 1   The Spill

Introduction

When Terry Carr wrote *Spill!*, he was an editorial writer for the *Anchorage Daily News.* His observations, research, and local reporting of the oil spill motivated him to share his story with a more global audience. He did this by writing an article for *Newsweek* (May, 1989). He also wrote a book for children. This was his first book.

Carr is primarily a journalist. His style of writing is very reflective of his background as a newspaper reporter. There are other types of journalists who write for specific periodicals or who are involved in broadcasting. Most journalists have one thing in common: their writing focuses on current, high-interest material.

This activity will motivate students to explore various types of journalism. At the end of the activity, they will write an article using a specific journalistic style.

Outcomes

1. To experience and understand the process and purpose of journalistic writing
2. To write an article using the principles and practices of known journalists

Materials

- newspapers
- periodicals
- "The Spill" worksheet

Procedure

1. Define journalism and the specific types of journalism that can be found in newspapers and periodicals or on television and radio. You might want to provide examples by having students read particular articles in local or national newspapers and periodicals or by having them listen to assigned broadcasts on television and radio. Discuss as a class what different journalistic forms have in common, and the type of material used to create each story or article.

2. Using Carr's book, return to the story of the *Exxon Valdez*. Review the information provided by the author and ask students to write their own article for a specific audience. Choices might include a local newspaper, a national periodical, or a local or national television broadcast. Have students use "The Spill" worksheet to complete their writing assignment.

Extending the Theme

- Have students identify topics of interest in their local community. Interview residents who might be able to address these topics at a local level. Organize a community talk show and invite these residents into the classroom as guest speakers. Students can act as the hosts for the guest speakers they have invited.

- Design and write an advertising campaign either for or against the utilization of oil for economic growth in Alaska.

• • • • • • • • • • • • • •

Activity 2　Speaking Out About Endangered Polar Regions

Introduction

Polar landscapes are increasingly being threatened by pollution, overhunting, and the exploitation of oil, gas, and minerals native to polar habitats.

Pollution may be the most difficult problem because some of its causes are integral to many people's lifestyles. Pesticides used in growing food, heavy metals produced by manufacturing processes, and increased rates of carbon dioxide expelled by motorists all play a role in altering polar ecosystems.

The overhunting of polar animals has received a great deal of public attention. Since Arctic territories go beyond national boundaries, controlling hunting practices is a political issue that must be regulated by international agreements.

The presence of the oil industry in polar regions has its benefits and drawbacks. The service it provides to Americans who drive automobiles and heat their homes with oil cannot be overlooked. The pursuit of oil and the impact it has had on nature, however, is a high price to pay to keep our automobiles on the road.

Similar to most issues, the dynamics of change created by pollution, overhunting, and oil exploitation in Alaska has found its way into the political arena. This activity will ask students to research and analyze the above concerns and to write a political speech that addresses controversies and resolutions for the future.

Outcomes

1. To research and analyze the dynamics of change facing polar regions
2. To develop and deliver a political speech that addresses the controversies and resolutions for future exploitation of Alaska's frontier

Materials

- reference materials specific to polar lands (See Polar Regions bibliography)
- "Speaking Out About Endangered Polar Regions" worksheet

Procedure

1. Most students have listened to local and national politicians speak out about the issues that concern their constituency. These politicians realize how important the relationship between political issues and public speaking is to their success as political leaders. Discuss various political leaders and how their public stand on specific issues may influence voters.

2. Tell students they are going to run for a political office in Alaska. The main issue of the campaign will focus on endangered habitats of the Arctic. Each student should research and write a speech that reflects their position on pollution, overhunting, and oil exploitation in Alaska. Have the class use the "Speaking Out About Endangered Polar Regions" worksheet to write their speeches.

3. Select four or five speeches that best address the campaign issue, and have those students deliver their speeches to the class. Based on the speeches, have students vote for a candidate. Voting should be done by secret ballot.

Extending the Theme

- Design and draw a political cartoon that deals with the issue of endangered polar environments.
- Ask each student to devise a slogan that supports their campaign position.

Pros and Cons of Mixing Oil and Nature

Nature:		Oil Industry:		People (Native Alaskans):	
Pros	Cons	Pros	Cons	Pros	Cons

Question: Do oil and nature mix? What would your position be on this issue?

Response: _____

_____

_____

_____

The Spill

You are a journalist. Your assignment is to write a story describing the oil spill created by the *Exxon Valdez*. Include information on the following: the collision, endangered wildlife, rescue and recovery, and prospects for the future.

Speaking Out About Endangered Polar Regions

You are running for political office. You must take a stand on the dangers threatening Arctic habitats. Write a speech outlining your position on this very crucial issue for Alaskans and their surrounding neighbors.

Although each illustration brings many changes in the window scene, there are also features of the original scene that remain the same. This activity will require students to observe new features of change, as well as features that remain the same or similar.

<table>
<tr><td>

Outcomes

1. To observe and record the new features of change seen through the window over a twenty-four-year period of time
2. To observe and record the features of the rural setting that remained the same or similar through a twenty-four-year period of time

</td><td>

Materials

- "Looking Out the Window" worksheet

</td></tr>
</table>

Procedure

1. Introduce the concept of change and how important it is to our everyday lives. Discuss how change influences our daily lives as well as our long-term plans and goals. Talk specifically about how changes in the environment can alter our lifestyles.

2. Share Baker's illustrated book with the class. Discuss changes in the wilderness scene as the young boy becomes a young man. Distribute the "Looking Out the Window" worksheet to each student. Return to Baker's illustrations. Show each illustration and have students record on their worksheets the differences and similarities of each changing scene.

3. When the worksheets are completed, discuss as a class the features of the original scene that changed and the features that remained the same or similar.

Extending the Theme

- Write an essay about how the scene from a window in your house has changed over time.
- Make a list of ten dreams you have for the wilderness environments of the world.

• • • • • • • • • • • • • • •

Activity 2   Starting Over

Introduction

When the young man in Baker's book grows up, he moves to the country with his small child. He began his life in the wilderness, and it is the lifestyle he wants for his child.

Like the young father looking out the window, many people around the world dream of an ideal lifestyle in the country. This dream, however, will become a reality for fewer people as the wilderness regions of the world become cities and suburbs. Our earth is indeed changing before our eyes.

One of the biggest challenges facing today's children is the realization that we must save our natural environments instead of destroying them. It is our job as parents and teachers to make sure they are ready to take on those challenges.

<table>
<tr><td>

Outcomes

1. To prepare students to think about the challenges facing them to protect the wilderness regions around the world
2. To predict what will happen to the young man's wilderness view as his child grows up to become an adult

</td><td>

Materials

- "Starting Over" worksheet

</td></tr>
</table>

Procedure

1. Review Baker's illustrations as a class. Go to the final illustration where the young man is looking out his window with his child in his arms. Have the class predict what the scene from the window will look like in another 5 years, 10 years, 15 years, and 20 years.

2. Using the "Starting Over" worksheet, ask students to write an essay describing how they think the young man can prevent his child's world from becoming the same world he left behind. Have students share their essays as a class.

Extending the Theme

- Write a greeting card to a friend with an illustration of a wilderness scene.
- Make a list of ten assumptions many people have about living in a wilderness environment.

Name: _____ **Date:** _____

From Wilderness to Skyscrapers

Record the characteristics of each stage of development in the process of changing wilderness to skyscrapers.

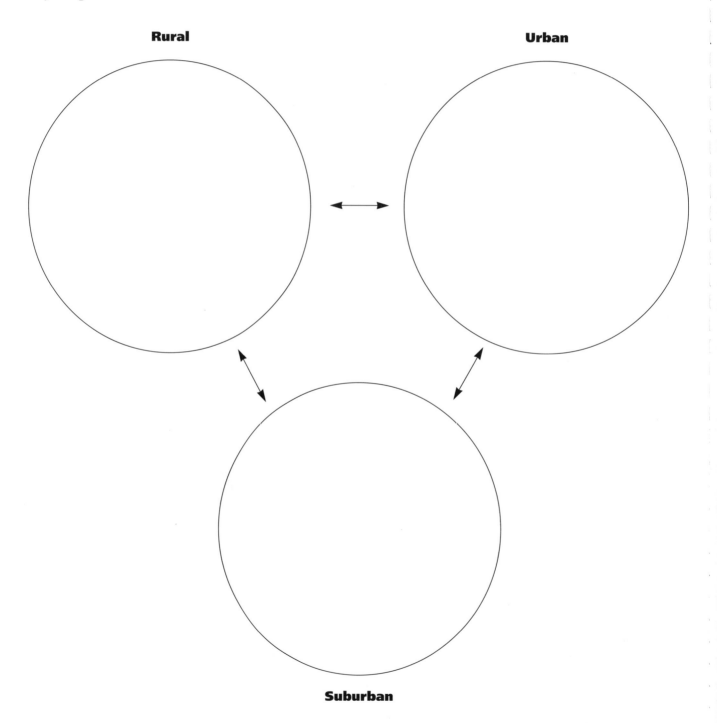

Rural

Urban

Suburban

Name: _____   **Date:** _____

Looking Out the Window

What were the similarities and differences of each changing scene over a period of twenty-four years?

Years	Similar	Different
Two		
Four		
Six		
Eight		
Ten		
Twelve		
Fourteen		
Sixteen		
Eighteen		
Twenty		
Twenty-two		
Twenty-four		

Name: _____ Date: _____

Starting Over

The concluding illustration of Baker's book finds the young man looking out the window with his small child in his arms. The scene is very much like the scene his mother had gazed at many years before. Describe how you think the young man can prevent his scene from becoming like the one he left behind.

Introduction

Stories keep cultures alive. Seeking to know more about the world beyond one's own culture, however, is an adventure children love to experience.

This theme will focus on a story about two Native Americans, one who takes the form of a crow, the other a weasel, and the adventures they share beyond the culture and lands of their people. It is a lesson about cultural diversity, and of the human obligation we have to help and respect people from all lands of the world.

Reading Activity
Crow and Weasel

by Barry Lopez (North Point Press, 1990)

Questions

1. How did Badger, Mouse, and Grizzly Bear help Crow and Weasel during their travels?
2. How did the Eskimos make Crow and Weasel feel at home?
3. What are the similarities and differences between Crow and Weasel's encounter with the Eskimos and Columbus's encounter with the Indians of the New World?
4. What did Crow and Weasel's adventures teach them about cultural diversity?
5. How did Crow and Weasel know that they were ready to return home?

Outcomes

1. To appreciate and understand that cultural differences do not necessitate cultural confrontation and conflict
2. To explore cultural diversity as a positive experience in the life cycle of all people

Materials

- "The Land That Binds Us" worksheet
- pencil

Discussion

Crow and Weasel, two very different characters, learn to respect and appreciate each other and the people, animals, and environments they encounter during their journey into foreign lands. They also learn some valuable lessons about friendship, thankfulness, courage, and the sharing of stories beyond one's own culture.

Discuss Crow and Weasel's travels into the diverse lands of the prairie, forests, and tundra. Who did they meet along the way, and how did these animals and people influence their friendship?

Using "The Land That Binds Us" worksheet, ask students to think about the characters in the story and to write three sentences describing each character. When the assignment is completed, have the class come together and discuss how the different qualities of each character influenced the events of Crow and Weasel's journey into foreign lands.

Interdisciplinary Activities

Famous Quotes of Crow and Weasel

Introduction

Crow and Weasel's adventures into foreign lands provided both characters with new experiences and knowledge beyond their Plains culture. As Crow and Weasel gained new knowledge, it would often be expressed in quotes by the author, Barry Lopez. Many of the quotes shared by the two main characters exemplified the lessons taught by their new cultural encounters.

Like Crow and Weasel, we all rely on quotes to communicate the essence and meaning of human experience. This activity will encourage children to understand the quotes used by Crow and Weasel and the relevance they had to their journey into foreign lands and cultures. It will also ask students to relate these quotes and lessons to their own lives.

Outcomes

1. To develop an awareness that what we say is a reflection of our daily experiences with the world around us
2. To appreciate the value of words in giving meaning and understanding to our lives

Materials

- "Famous Quotes of Crow and Weasel" worksheet
- a book of quotes for all occasions.

Procedure

1. Begin by discussing what quotes are and how they are used in everyday life. Provide examples of common quotes and ask students to elaborate on their meaning.

2. Using the "Famous Quotes of Crow and Weasel" worksheet, have the class chart what they believe to be important quotes expressed by the characters of the story. These quotes should lend insight into the lessons learned by Crow and Weasel as they explored new lands and people.

3. When the webbing chart is complete, ask students to think about the relationship between the quotes and the lessons. Is one quote connected to another quote in terms of meaning? Is one lesson connected to another lesson? How? Are the collective quotes and lessons interdependent? How does that interdependency apply to our everyday lives? How does it apply to the people we meet in life who have a culture different from our own?

4. To culminate this activity, have each student take a quote from one of the characters in the book and illustrate it using their own life experience. Compile illustrations into a class booklet titled "Famous Quotes of Crow and Weasel."

Extending the Theme

- Have students select a culture they would like to visit and create a quote about a lesson they might expect to learn through their contact with that culture.

- Ask children to illustrate a story they would like to keep in their memory to pass onto the people they meet in life.

Discovering New Lands

Introduction

Crow and Weasel experienced many adventures as they traveled north into unknown territory. They saw land, animals, and people foreign to their culture. They tasted the meat of an animal distant to their land and embraced people and animals they, at first encounter, feared.

This activity will focus on the ecological diversity of Crow and Weasel's journey. It is designed to allow children to appreciate the wonders of diverse environments.

Outcomes

1. To provide children with an opportunity to explore different environments
2. To develop the awareness that all environments deserve our concern and respect

Materials

- brown grocery bags
- markers
- crayons
- natural materials (leaves, feathers, pebbles, etc.)
- "Discovering New Lands" worksheet

Procedure

1. Using a map of the United States, have students locate the ecological zones traveled by Crow and Weasel.

2. Distribute the "Discovering New Lands" worksheet. Ask students to describe or illustrate the sequence of Crow and Weasel's journey. When they have completed their worksheets, have the students come together and discuss the different landscapes and adventures of each traveled land.

3. Culminate the activity by making banners that represent the sights, sounds, tastes, and smells of an environment traveled by Crow and Weasel. Students should begin by addressing questions such as: What do the animals of the habitat look like? How would they feel to touch? What would be the smells, tastes and sounds of the flowers, forests, rivers, and plant life? Help children with their sensory exploration by reading poetry that describes nature or by having them find books that focus on the illustration of nature.

4. When students have completed their sensory investigation, they are ready to begin their banner. Two students can share one grocery bag. Cut the two larger sides of the bag so that they have two banners. Fringe one end of each banner and fold the other. Leave enough room in the fold to insert a piece of wood or yarn. Children can either draw scenes or arrange natural materials on their banner. Create a "Nature Display" in the classroom by hanging completed banners.

Extending the Theme

- Explore why Crow and Weasel were chosen by the author to be the main characters. What characteristics do crows and weasels have in common with the main characters of the story? Why do Native Americans tend to personify animals in their stories about human experience?

- Learn more about the Eskimos known as the Inuit by reading *Arctic Memories* by Normee Ekoomiak (Henry Holt and Company, 1988).

The Land That Binds Us

Write three sentences describing the following characters in the book *Crow and Weasel.*

Character: Crow

1. _____

2. _____

3. _____

Character: Weasel

1. _____

2. _____

3. _____

Character: Badger

1. _____

2. _____

3. _____

Character: Grizzly Bear

1. _____

2. _____

3. _____

Characters: Eskimos

1. _____

2. _____

3. _____

Character: Mouse

1. _____

2. _____

3. _____

Name: _____   **Date:** _____

Famous Quotes of Crow and Weasel

Record five quotes stated by either Crow or Weasel. Describe the lesson that each quote provided.

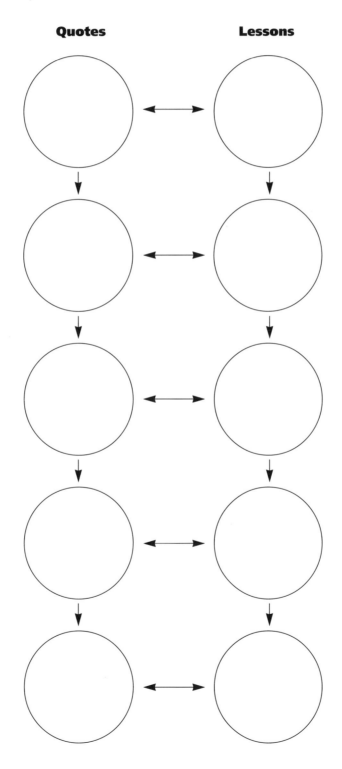

Quotes   **Lessons**

Name: _____ **Date:** _____

Discovering New Lands

Describe or illustrate the different lands traveled by Crow and Weasel.

Plains:

Forests:

Tundra:

From Cornfield to Forest

Introduction

Joe McCrephy abandoned his Ohio cornfield to go west to Wyoming. During his absence, the unplanted field returned to its natural state. Wildflowers blossomed, meadowlarks sang, and saplings grew into trees taller than the old barn that had once towered over the working cornfield.

After fifty years, Joe returns to his cornfield and walks through the woods that were once carefully planned rows of corn. He carves his initials on the old barn door and lays down in the shade nearby to take a summer nap. Joe McCrephy, like his cornfield, has gone through many changes, and the reader cannot help but wonder what Joe is thinking as he slumbers off to sleep on the memories of his Ohio cornfield.

Reading Activity
McCrephy's Field

by Christopher and Lynne Myers (Houghton Mifflin, 1991)

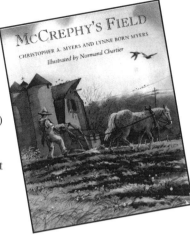

Questions

1. What changes evolved on Joe's cornfield during the first year of his absence?
2. Why did Joe abandon his cornfield?
3. What did the cornfield look like after fifty years?
4. Why do you think Joe returned to his cornfield?
5. Why did Joe carve his initials on the old barn door?

Outcomes

1. To explore the evolution of an unplanted cornfield over a period of fifty years
2. To critically evaluate the pros and cons of restoring farmland to its natural state

Materials

- "From Field to Forest" worksheet
- pencil

Discussion

While Joe was gone, McCrephy's field went through some major changes. Over the course of fifty years, the changing supply of food and shelter gave way to a variety of new plant and animal residents.

The Myerses explain the changes that occurred on Joe's farm during his absence in five specific time intervals. Using the "From Field to Forest" worksheet, ask students to plot the changing plants and animals that inhabited the cornfield as it made its way into becoming a forest.

When students have completed the chart, have them think about why Joe McCrephy said to his cornfield "You and I have gone through some changes." Students can discuss why they think he made this comment by answering the question on the bottom of the "From Field to Forest" worksheet.

Interdisciplinary Activities

Activity 1   The Pros and Cons of Restoring World Environments

Introduction

Joe McCrephy did not leave his cornfield because he wanted it to return to a natural state. Many people around the world, however, are growing increasingly concerned about the consequences of human exploitation in pristine world environments. They feel that the consequences of exploitation necessitate a global policy for the protection of our world's environments. These consequences include: depletion of natural resources, air and water pollution caused by increased industrialization, and extinction of many plant and animal populations.

People supporting increased human exploitation of world environments argue that it is necessary to secure jobs, food supplies, and natural resources for expanding world populations.

The decision to restore or exploit world environments will quite likely become a major global question for the children of this generation. It is important for them to learn as much as they can about the dynamics of this crucial issue.

This activity will encourage students to think about the pros and cons of restoring world environments. It will also allow them to develop their positions as future decision-makers and residents of a world system.

Outcomes

1. To gather information, research and analyze the pros and cons of restoring world environments back to their natural state
2. To develop a position concerning the issues pertinent to the restoration of world environments

Materials

- reference materials relevant to the world's environments (refer to the bibliographies for the Regions of the World)
- "The Pros and Cons of Restoring World Environments" worksheet

Procedure

1. Introduce the issue of restoring world environments by using several reference sources to illustrate the diversity of natural environments around the world. Discuss how these environments have been exploited by both animal and human populations. Ask the class to think about possible concerns they might have for the future of specific environments.

2. Divide the class into six groups and assign each group a world region (polar, rain forests, deserts, grasslands, seashores, mountains).

3. Using the chart found on "The Pros and Cons of Restoring World Environments" worksheet, ask each group to investigate the pros and cons of restoration for their specific environment.

4. When students have completed their charts, have them come together as a class and report on the pros and cons of restoring each world environment. Culminate the activity by asking students to answer the question on the bottom of the "Pros and Cons" worksheet. This question requires them to choose a world environment they feel is in the most need of saving, and to develop a plan of action that would convince others of this need.

Extending the Theme

- Design environmental awards and present them to students, teachers, or parents who are caught doing something good for their natural environment.
- Write and illustrate an ad for a magazine or newspaper that supports saving a specific world environment.

· · · · · · · · · · · · · ·

Activity 2   Around the World in Fifty Years

Introduction

Like Joe's cornfield, the passing of years bring change to all living things. Youth can become old age, life can become death, and knowledge can become wisdom.

Taking time out to contemplate our world fifty years from now encourages us to think critically about ourselves and what we want for our global future. This activity will ask students to think about the world they foresee, and to relate that world to themselves.

Outcomes

1. To critically assess the future of our world
2. To contemplate where and what we will be fifty years from now

Materials

- *Oh, the Places You'll Go!* by Dr. Seuss (Random House, 1990)
- "Around the World in Fifty Years" worksheet

Procedure

1. Introduce the concept of change over the years by reading *Oh, the Places You'll Go!* by Dr. Seuss. Ask the class to discuss the places they'll go to in the future, and what they think the world will be like in another fifty years.

2. Ask students to pretend that they and the world around them is fifty years older. Using a world map or globe, have them travel to different parts of the world and describe some of the changes that have taken place since their youth. The "Around the World in Fifty Years" worksheet will help students complete the assignment.

3. When the class has finished the assignment, ask them to share their views of the future world with other classmates.

Extending the Theme

• Make a list of fifty places you would like to visit in the next fifty years. Give a reason for wanting to go to each place.

• Design a calendar using "World Regions" as a theme.

Name: _____ **Date:** _____

From Cornfield to Forest

Plot the changes Joe's field went through during the fifty years of his absence.

	1 Year	5 Years	10 Years	25 Years	50 Years
Plants					
Animals					

Question: When Joe McCrephy returned to his field, he said "You and I have gone through some changes." Discuss why you think he made this comment.

Response: _____

_____

_____

_____

_____

The Pros and Cons of Restoring World Environments

Pros	Cons

Question: Which world environment do you feel is in the most need of returning to its natural state? How would you get more people to realize the urgency in saving this environment?

Response: _____

_____

_____

_____

_____

Around the World in Fifty Years

You are now fifty years older and the world has changed a great deal. Using a globe or world map, discuss some of the changes that have taken place since your childhood.

Talking Walls Around the World

Introduction

People around the world build walls for many different purposes. Some walls are designed to keep people in, others are designed to keep invaders or strangers out (The Great Wall of China and The Berlin Wall, that was opened 1989). The Vietnam War Memorial is a wall that was created to honor Americans who died or were missing as a result of the Vietnam War. The Western Wall, located in the old city of Jerusalem, is a sacred and holy wall to Jews around the world. The cliff and cave walls of Australia are home to many paintings done by Australia's Aborigine people. They used these paintings to communicate with each other and to record their history.

Do walls talk? If they do, what do they tell us? Students will enjoy exploring different walls around the world, and learning about the diverse cultures who made these walls famous.

Reading Activity

Talking Walls

by Margy Burns Knight (Tilbury House, 1992)

Questions

1. Who found the Lascaux Cave (France), and how was it used by its original inhabitants?
2. Why is the Western Wall so important to Jews around the world?
3. How do walls tell us about the cultures who created them?
4. What was the purpose of the Berlin Wall and why was it torn down on November 9, 1989?
5. Which wall would you choose to visit and why.

Outcomes

1. To investigate and explore fourteen walls around the world, all created by diverse cultures and for varying reasons
2. To research and analyze the relationship between cultures around the world and the walls they build

Materials

- world map
- "Walls Around the World" worksheet
- pencil

Discussion

The walls described by the author, Margy Knight, are located in different regions around the world. Encouraging students to use their imaginations to climb, touch, and explore these very different walls will lead them to a better understanding of the cultures who conceived them. It will also make them realize that although the walls are culturally distinct, they share similar purposes. Listening to what the walls tell us, therefore, is an important lesson for the understanding of worldwide human behavior, expressed in cultural disguises.

While reading the book *Talking Walls*, have the class locate the walls being discussed on a world map. Using the "Walls Around the World" worksheet, have students write the name of the wall next to the appropriate number.

While labeling the different walls on the world map, ask students to discuss the culture responsible for building the wall, and their reasons behind its construction.

Interdisciplinary Activities

Activity 1   A Wall Is Born

Introduction

Many cultures express their identity and beliefs through the creation of walls. Some walls are designed out of fear, hate, or safety; others out of love and respect for specific cultural traditions. The Berlin Wall, for example, was a structure created out of fear. The Vietnam War Memorial, on the other hand, was a wall honoring the cultural tradition of loyalty and service to one's country.

There are many walls waiting to be built. This activity will ask students to identify a cultural value, belief, or historical event that might stimulate them to start building a wall of their own.

Outcomes

1. To determine one value, belief, or historical event that could motivate a cultural group to build a wall
2. To design and illustrate a wall based on one cultural value, belief, or historical event

Materials

• "A Wall is Born" worksheet

Procedure

1. Review the walls discussed by Knight, and the values, beliefs and historical events that motivated their construction. Encourage students to think about a value, belief, or historical event that might inspire them to build a wall. Guide them in creating walls that project a positive message for all people of the world. Examples might include walls that support world peace, protection of endangered animals, or preservation of natural environments.

2. Distribute the "A Wall Is Born" worksheet. Have students record the name of their wall, its location, and the purpose for its construction. Ask them to illustrate their wall using the same worksheet.

3. Students will enjoy sharing their finished walls as a class.

Extending the Theme

• Have students make a model or diorama of their wall.

• Ask students to write a "how-to-do-it" speech about the construction of their wall. Share the speeches as a class.

• • • • • • • • • • • • • •

Activity 2   A World Without Walls

Introduction

Can you imagine a world without walls? There would be no walls to divide us, to imprison us, or to inspire us. What would that world be like?

This activity will ask students to think about how walls are used in our everyday lives. These walls are not necessarily the famous walls described by Knight. They can be walls of any kind, that are constructed for the same reasons that motivated the famous walls of the world.

Outcomes

1. To determine how walls influence our everyday lives
2. To contemplate a world without walls

Materials

• "A World Without Walls" worksheet

Procedure

1. Review the location and historical events around the creation of the Berlin Wall. Discuss, as a class, how this massive wall influenced the daily lives of the people of West and East Berlin. Compare and contrast the meaning of walls among the Australian Aborigines or the Native Americans of Taos, New Mexico, with those of the people of West and East Berlin.

2. Encourage students to think about the walls that give meaning to their daily lifestyle. These walls do not have to be local or national structures. They can be imaginary walls we create as individuals to keep us secure from the things we fear in our everyday lives.

3. Ask students to write an essay describing what they think the world would be like without walls. Use the worksheet titled, "A World Without Walls," to help them complete the assignment. You might want to culminate this activity by having students share their essays.

Extending the Theme

• Some people talk to walls. Ask individual students to choose a wall. Go around the classroom having each student share what they would say to that wall.

• The Berlin Wall was torn down on November 9, 1989. Write its epitaph.

Walls Around the World

Using the world map below, identify numerically the walls around the world.

1. _____   8. _____

2. _____   9. _____

3. _____   10. _____

4. _____   11. _____

5. _____   12. _____

6. _____   13. _____

7. _____   14. _____

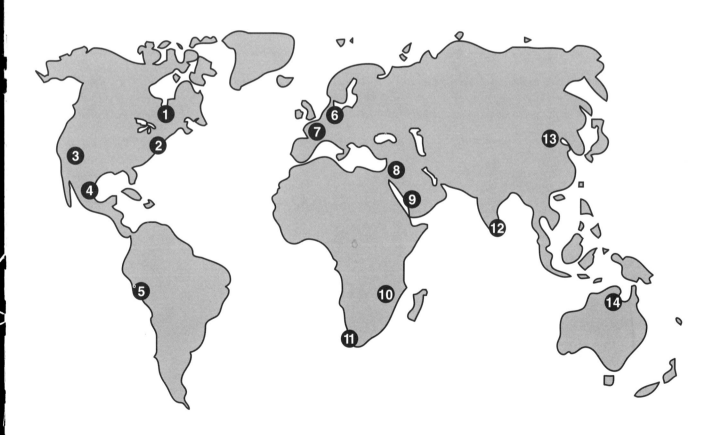

Name: _____ **Date:** _____

A Wall is Born

Name: _____

Location: _____

_____

Purpose: _____

_____

Illustration:

A World Without Walls

Imagine a world without walls. What would it be like?

Introduction

It has been 500 years since Columbus sailed the ocean blue and the story of his exploration into a new world has captured the hearts of generations of schoolchildren. What many students do not realize, however, is that Columbus did not "discover" America.

There is evidence that before Columbus, Vikings explored the land we now call North America, and that upon the arrival of Columbus, Indians were there to greet the mysterious "white men." The Taino, who welcomed Columbus to their land, have remained historically silent. Their story of cultural contact, conflict, and change is the focus of this theme. It is a story all children should hear.

Reading Activity

Encounter

by Jane Yolen (Harcourt Brace Jovanovich, 1992)

Questions

1. The main character in this book is a child. How was his dream or vision a warning to Taino?
2. Why did Jane Yolen choose to tell this story through the vision of a child?
3. How were Columbus and his crew described by the Taino?
4. What changes in Taino culture came about as a result of Columbus's visit?
5. What warning does the old man pass on to the children and people of every land?

Outcomes

1. To have children develop an appreciation and respect for the Taino
2. To investigate and analyze the sociocultural and technological dimensions of contact between Native Americans and Europeans

Materials

- "Culture Contact" worksheet
- pencil

Discussion

The encounter of two very different cultures usually creates a setting for social and cultural change. Jane Yolen, in her description of the historical events surrounding Columbus's encounter with the Taino, chooses to tell her story of cultural contact through the feelings and fears of a young Taino boy.

The young boy listens carefully for the signs and warnings of change facing his people. He acknowledges the white explorers as men, but realizes the vast differences that separate them as people. The chief of the Taino, on the other hand, feels they must be generous with their visitors in exchange for a few small trinkets. He keeps insisting that it is childlike fear that is keeping the young boy from trusting the white strangers.

Using the "Culture Contact" worksheet, ask students to compare the cultures of the Taino and Columbus through the characters created by Yolen.

Discuss how Jane Yolen used the vision of a young child to tell this moving story of cultural contact and change.

From *Discovering World Cultures Through Literature* published by GoodYearBooks. Copyright © 1995 Gerry Edwards.

Interdisciplinary Activities

Activity 1 Before and After Columbus

Introduction

Columbus landed on San Salvatore on October 12, 1492. The Taino welcomed the white strangers by having a feast. They exchanged gifts and Columbus left with dreams of gold and Indian slaves. The Taino also dreamed. Their dreams were of winged ships and metal spears. Little did they realize how much Columbus's visit would change their lives and the land they so greatly cherished.

The dynamics of change between Columbus and the Taino is an important lesson for children to explore. It will allow them to see a view of the world that is constantly changing—a view which will better prepare them for the environmental and cultural challenges they'll face in the future, a view which will better prepare them for the future of their own cultural survival.

Outcomes

1. To investigate and analyze the cultural contact between Columbus and the Taino
2. To evaluate the cultural change from two perspectives; that of Columbus and that of the Taino
3. To recognize the relationship between environmental development and cultural change

Materials

- "Before and After Columbus" worksheet

Procedure

1. Have class brainstorm the lifestyle of the Taino before and after Columbus. Distribute the "Before and After Columbus" worksheet to help students complete the assignment.

2. Once students have an understanding of the contact environment, have them write a reaction essay describing their response to this chapter of American history. Use the following questions to focus their writing:

   a. Was Columbus an explorer who sought exploitation of the Taino and their land? Explain your answer.

   b. How and why were the Taino victims of this exploitation?

   c. Did the Taino benefit from the exploration of Columbus? Explain your answer.

   d. What lessons can we learn from Columbus and the Taino people about cultural diversity and social change?

   e. How can we apply those lessons to the global world we live in today?

3. Have students share their essays as a class and discuss the diverse feelings generated by the encounter of Columbus and the Taino.

Extending the Theme

- Compare the stone technology of the Taino with the metal technology of Columbus. What influence would the shift in technology have upon the Taino and their environment?

- Investigate Indian slavery. Was Columbus the only explorer to make the Indians slaves or were there others who followed in his footsteps? What was the purpose of slavery? How did it benefit Columbus?

• • • • • • • • • • • • • •

| Activity 2 | **Following The Trail of Famous Explorers** |

Introduction

Through the words of Jane Yolen, children can experience a "native" perspective of European contact with Indian populations. The contact between Columbus and the Taino changed the Taino world forever. The pre-contact, post-contact experiences of the Taino is similar to the experiences of many other groups of Native Americans.

This activity will follow the trail of famous explorers in relation to the changes that took place within the "contact environment." These changes altered the beliefs and lifestyles of many Native Americans and left them subordinate and dependent on their European visitors.

Outcomes

1. To investigate and analyze the processes of change in the pre-contact and post-contact environments of the New World

2. To appreciate and understand the cultural contact of two diverse populations as a process, not an event

Materials

• "Following the Trail of Famous Explorers" worksheet

Procedure

1. Begin this activity by taking students on an exploration of their playground or schoolyard. Have them discover an object and describe it in writing. When all students have completed the exploration of their discovery, return to the classroom to discuss and share the experience of being an explorer. The following questions will help initiate discussion:

   a. How does it feel to make a discovery?

   b. How do you think Columbus felt when he "discovered" the Taino?

   c. If you could rewrite the story of Columbus, what would you change?

   d. Was your discovery changed by your exploration?

   e. As an explorer, do you have a responsibility to your discovery? Explain your answer.

2. Divide students into groups and assign each group an explorer. Have students collect information about their explorers: What country sponsored the exploration? What did the explorer discover? What Native Americans inhabited the discovered region? What was the natural environment of the area, and how was it changed by European contact? How were the Indians of the region changed? Were there similarities and differences between the Taino and other Indian groups who experienced contact?

3. Once students have completed their reports, come together as a class and plot the name of each group's explorer, area of exploration, and native populations he or she contacted by using the "Following the Trail of Famous Explorers" worksheet.

4. While the students are working on their charts, have them critically discuss the process of cultural change through the contact of diverse cultures. Make sure they understand that the contact environment created by European exploration was a process and not a series of unrelated events.

Extending the Theme

• Students will enjoy playing the game "Guess Who I Am?" The class is divided into two groups. Each group gets a turn to present three facts about a famous explorer. If the opposing group guesses the correct answer after the first clue, they get three points; second clue, two points; and third clue, one point. The group with the most points wins the game.

• The Taino referred to Columbus's sailing vessels as "winged ships." What would their response have been to the space vehicles of today? Students will find it fascinating to explore the technological changes in travel between the time of Columbus and today.

120

Name: _____ Date: _____

Culture Contact

Plot the cultural beliefs and values of the Taino and Columbus as portrayed through the characters created by Jane Yolen.

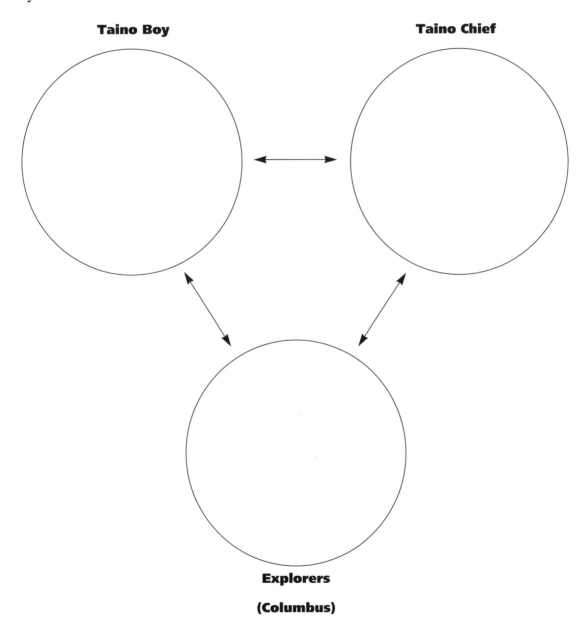

Name: _____ **Date:** _____

Before and After Columbus

Record the qualities of the Taino lifestyle before and after Columbus.

Before	After

Name: _____ Date: _____

Following the Trail of Famous Explorers

Create a chart of explorers, areas they explored, people they encountered, and cultural changes they initiated by their contact with native peoples.

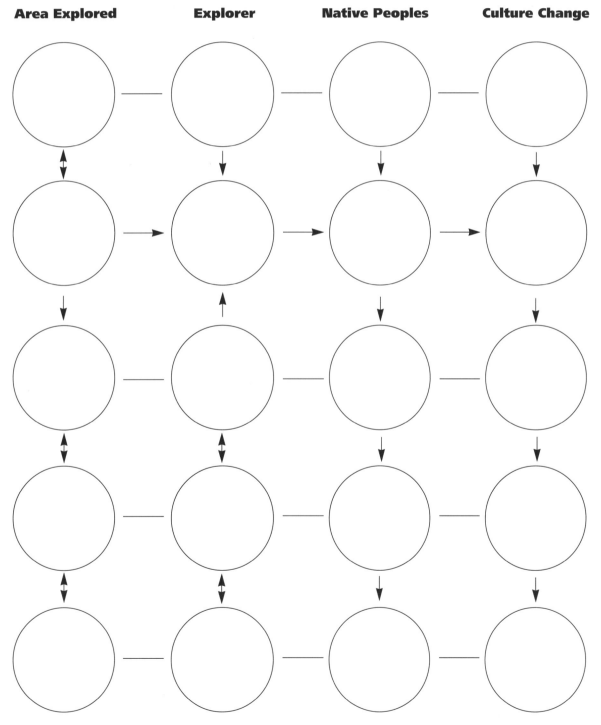

Introduction

It was early in the morning on August 6, 1945, and the world was at war. The sirens of the city of Hiroshima, Japan, warned of approaching danger. Junko Morinoto, a young Japanese girl, had stayed home from school that day and was in her room talking to her sister. The sirens stopped and the sounds of a plane seemed distant. Without further warning, an explosion of sound and fire changed Junko's life forever. She watched as her city and her people were devastated by the world's first nuclear attack.

Junko's message to parents and their children is a simple one: learn from the mistakes made by those who came before us, and place a high value on all life.

Reading Activity
My Hiroshima

by Junko Morimoto (Viking, 1987)

Questions

1. What was Junko's life like before the dropping of the atomic bomb?
2. How did Junko's life begin to change in response to the war, before the atomic bomb?
3. How did Junko describe the city of Hiroshima immediately following the bomb's explosion?
4. What role did Junko's family play in her survival?
5. What is the message Junko is giving to parents, teachers, and children of today's world?

Outcomes

1. To empathize with Junko Morimoto's childhood memory of the first atomic bomb attack
2. To relate Junko Morimoto's memory to our own lives, both present and future

Materials

- "Victims of War" worksheet
- pencil

Discussion

Hiroshima, a city embraced by green mountains and picturesque rivers, was the first to experience the destruction of an atomic bomb. Junko Morimoto, a child growing up in Hiroshima during the war, shares her memories of home, school, and family before and after that fateful day when her world was changed forever.

Ask students to recall Junko's memories of her home, school, city, and friends before the day of the explosion. How were things beginning to change prior to the dropping of the bomb? Discuss how Junko was a victim of a war she had no control over, and how children are often the victims of war instead of the policymakers who deemed the war necessary.

Using the "Victims of War" worksheet, have students record the changes that took place in Junko's life before and after the bombing of Hiroshima. Ask them to also answer the question: What is Junko's message for today's children, their parents, and their teachers?

When students have completed the assignment, have them share their feelings about Junko's experience to their own fears of existing or future wars.

Interdisciplinary Activities

| Activity 1 | War And Peace |

Introduction

There are many different types of wars and many various reasons given for declaring war. All wars, however, are born out of human conflict. Acting out conflict, regardless of its origins, brings devastation and death to its human and nonhuman victims. Peace, a product of human respect for all life, is the hope for our future. Is it an impossible dream or is it within our reality?

Outcomes

1. To investigate and analyze the concepts of war and peace
2. To apply the concepts of war and peace to the future of a global society

Materials

• "War or Peace" worksheet

Procedure

1. Have each student bring into school a book or a magazine or newspaper article that describes a conflict or war situation somewhere in the world. It can be a historical conflict or one that is taking place currently.

2. Using a world map or globe, define the scenes of conflict in various locations around the world. Discuss the issues involved in their warfare, and the reasons they cited for acting out their differences.

3. Knowing the background of each conflict, ask students what they would have done to encourage a peaceful ending to the same set of circumstances. Were there situations when war could have been avoided? Were there times when peace was only possible through acting out conflict?

4. Using the "War or Peace" worksheet, ask each student to choose and describe two world conflicts, one they support and another one they feel should have been resolved using a more peaceful approach. Share and discuss essays as a class.

Extending the Theme

• Divide students into two groups and have one group debate the merits of war, the other the merits of peace.

• Make a list of ten proverbs that support peace over war.

● ● ● ● ● ● ● ● ● ● ● ● ● ●

Activity 2   The Environment of War

Introduction

The devastation of war is usually expressed in human terms. We tend to forget that the natural environment, supporting human life, is also a victim of war's destructive process.

When we look at places like Hiroshima, we must also wonder what the cost of life was to our natural environments. What influence did the bomb have on the plant and animal life of the region? How did the waters of the seven rivers flowing through Hiroshima recover the bomb's powerful pollution and radiation remains?

Like Hiroshima, many other natural environments of the world are endangered due to the pursuit of human conflict and warfare. Addressing this issue is crucial to our function as parents and teachers of the children who will determine the future for both our human and natural worlds.

Outcomes

1. To appreciate the relationship between global warfare and endangered natural environments
2. To understand that global peace is directly linked to preserving humanity and natural environments

Materials

• "The Environment of War" worksheet

Procedure

1. Discuss how warfare influences different features of the natural environment. Use Hiroshima as an example. Ask students to compare or contrast other environments that were endangered in response to human conflict. Examples might include the American bison of the Great Plains, the debris-infested air of Pearl Harbor, or the polluted waters of Kuwait.

2. Using "The Environment of War" worksheet, ask students to identify how various features of the environment become endangered by warfare. This activity can be culminated by having students draw illustrations of "The Environment of War."

Extending the Theme

• Pretend you are a newscast reporter describing the bombing of Hiroshima to your viewers.

• Write a recipe for global peace.

Name: _____ Date: _____

Victims of War

How did the following change in Junko Morimoto's life after the bombing of Hiroshima?

Home: _____

_____

_____

City of Hiroshima: _____

_____

_____

Banks of River: _____

_____

_____

Family: _____

_____

_____

School: _____

_____

_____

Question: What is Junko Morimoto's message for today's children and their parents? _____

_____

_____

_____

_____

War or Peace?

Describe a war you would support. Give reasons why you would support it.

Describe a war you would not support. Give reasons why you would not support it.

Name: _____ Date: _____

The Environment of War

How are the following features of our natural environments around the world influenced by warfare?

Land:

Water:

Air:

Plants:

Animals:

Exploring the Moon on the Back of a Turtle

Introduction

Native Americans have always watched the natural world surrounding them with wonder and respect. Looking up at the sky, they have noticed that the moon changes over a period of twenty-nine days, and that there are thirteen cycles of the moon in one year. Native Americans relate these thirteen cycles to the seasons of the year.

Many Native American cultures believe that the turtle, having thirteen scales, possesses the mystery of each moon on the shell of its back. Joseph Bruchac and Jonathan London explore the thirteen moons on turtle's back by sharing one moon story from thirteen distinctive Native American groups in various regions of North America. Their stories, expressed as poems, communicate a message of beauty and wonder for all cultures of the world to enjoy.

Reading Activity

The Thirteen Moons on Turtle's Back

by Joseph Bruchac and Jonathan London (Philomel, 1992)

Questions

1. How do Native Americans pass the moon stories from generation to generation?
2. What do the moon stories tell us about the seasons of the year?
3. Why does the turtle have thirteen scales?
4. How are animals described in the moon stories?
5. Why are animals so important to the traditional lifestyle of Native Americans?

Outcomes

1. To experience the bonding many world cultures feel between themselves and their natural environment
2. To appreciate the cultural diversity of Native Americans as expressed through the thirteen moon cycles and the seasons of the year

Materials

- "Thirteen Moons" worksheet
- pencil

Discussion

According to Native American legend, each of the thirteen moons has its own name and its own story. From the Moon of the Popping Trees to the Moon of the Falling Leaves, the natural world is a source of miracles and amazement. Passing these stories down from generation to generation allows all people to understand the mysteries of the world around them.

Using the "Thirteen Moons" worksheet, review the moons discussed by Bruchac and London. Ask students to record the name of each moon, along with a short description of why it was given that particular name. Discuss how the thirteen moons relate to the seasons of the year, and why Native Americans traditionally believe that it is the turtle who holds the secrets to understanding the moon's mysteries and power.

Interdisciplinary Activities

Activity 1 ## Exploring the Moon Through Science and Myth

Introduction

Modern science has made it possible for humans to land on the moon. Such an accomplishment has generated a feeling that we can control the natural world through scientific experimentation and exploration.

Many people of the world, however, continue to value and respect the relationship between humans and nature. These people explain the wonders of nature through the legends, myths, and observations passed down to them by their ancestors. Most people combine the achievements of science and the folklore of traditional myths and legends to help them understand more completely their relationship with the natural world.

This activity asks students to study the moon by comparing and contrasting theories of science with those of selected world myths and legends.

Outcomes

1. To investigate the contributions of science that have revealed many mysteries of the moon
2. To gain an appreciation and respect for the role traditional myths and legends have played in our understanding of the moon
3. To compare and contrast scientific theories with of traditional myths and legends

Materials

- "Exploring the Moon Through Science and Myth" worksheet

Procedure

1. Discuss as a class the different ways science has helped us to better understand the earth's moon. Focus on achievements related to space exploration (Neil Armstrong, David Scott, Buzz Aldrin, Jim Irwin, and the Apollo explorations).
2. Ask students to think of legends and myths used by various cultures around the world to explain the mysteries of the moon. They can begin with *Thirteen Moons on Turtle's Back* by Bruchac and London.
3. Divide the class into six groups; three groups should be assigned to researching scientific contributions, and the other three groups to collecting myths and legends from specific world cultures.
4. Allow students two to three days to collect their data and organize it as a group. When all groups have completed the assignment, have the class come together and record their findings. The "Exploring the Moon Through Science and Myth" worksheet can be used for this activity.

Extending the Theme

- Research a famous astronaut and write a legend based on his explorations.
- Investigate the origins of such phrases as "the man in the moon" and the "moon is made of cheese." Develop contemporary phrases that are more appropriate to the moon as we know it.

Activity 2 ## The Changing Faces of the Moon

Introduction

The moon's face is always changing as it moves through its monthly cycle. Starting as a new moon, it changes to become a crescent moon, a half moon, a gibbous moon, and then finally a full moon. This five-phased sequence of the moon's cycle takes approximately two weeks, during which time we refer to the moon as waxing.

kind

During the third and the fourth weeks of its monthly cycle, the full moon changes into a gibbous moon, then a half moon and a crescent moon, and finally seems to disappear, only to reappear as a new moon. We refer to the moon during these five phases as waning.

Watching the moon wax and wane during its monthly cycle can be an exciting project for people of all ages. As the moon phases in and phases out, children will especially enjoy the moon's "game" of "Now you see me, now you don't."

Outcomes

1. To observe and identify the different phases of the moon's monthly cycle
2. To record and illustrate the different phases of the moon's monthly cycle

Materials

- "The Changing Faces of the Moon" worksheet
- *Why Does the Moon Change Shape?* by Isaac Asimov (Gareth Stevens, 1991), or a similar reference book that will help students become familiar with the moon's monthly cycle

Procedure

1. Ask "How does the moon change shape each month?" Allow students to discuss how the moon changes and why. You might want to illustrate this process by using a flashlight and a round object such as a ball. Explain that when the light from the sun (flashlight) shines on a round object (the moon), half of the object will be in light and the other half in shadow. During the moon's monthly cycle, we see different amounts of light on the moon's face, depending on the sunlight being reflected back to the earth as moonlight (full moon—full face; new moon—full shadow).

2. Review the names of the phases of the moon and what each looks like (full, crescent, half, gibbous, new moon). Distribute "The Changing Faces of the Moon" worksheet and have students number the calendar for the 29 days they will observe the moon's cycle. Allow them to take their calendars home and record and illustrate what they see each day. They should label what they illustrate.

3. After the calendars are completed, have students review their data to see if their observations were consistent with the pattern originally discussed in class.

Extending the Theme

- Learn more about the moon by writing letters to the following agencies:

  National Space Society
  600 Maryland Avenue SW
  Washington, D.C. 20024

  NASA Kennedy Space Center
  Educational Services Office
  Kennedy Space Center
  Florida 32899

- Most calendars have twelve months and are based on the seasons of the year. Lunar calendars are based on the phases of the moon, and each month begins with the new moon. The Islamic and Hebrew calendars are examples of lunar calendars. Using these examples, compare the similarities and differences between the two different types of calendars. An excellent reference to begin your comparison is *Calendar Art: Thirteen Days, Weeks, Months, and Years from Around the World* by Leonard Fisher (Macmillan, 1987).

Name: _____ Date: _____

Thirteen Moons

First Moon _____
_____

Second Moon _____

Third Moon _____
_____

Fourth Moon _____
_____

Fifth Moon _____
_____

Sixth Moon _____
_____

Seventh Moon _____
_____

Eighth Moon _____
_____

Ninth Moon _____
_____

Tenth Moon _____
_____

Eleventh Moon _____
_____

Twelfth Moon _____
_____

Thirteenth Moon _____
_____

Name: _____ **Date:** _____

Exploring the Moon Through Science and Myth

Identify the different ways science and world legends help us to better understand the earth's moon.

Science   **World Legends**

The Changing Faces of the Moon

Over a twenty-nine day period, observe the different phases of the moon. Label and illustrate them in the appropriate calendar box.

Exploring the Sun Through African Legend

Introduction

The grasslands of the Maasai have been hit by a harsh and relentless drought. The birds appeal to the small Bat to find a way of bringing rain back to their precious homeland.

The small Bat goes to the Moon, Stars, Clouds, and Winds for help, but without success. Finally, she pleads with the burning Sun. The Sun agrees to bring rain to the dying land in return for a special promise.

This African legend, told by Tololwa Mollel, recounts the tale of a small Bat who tries to keep his promise to the Sun, and what happens to him when his efforts fail. This legend gives children one culture's perspective of why bats are nocturnal animals and why the sun pauses before setting below the horizon.

Reading Activity

A Promise to the Sun

by Tololwa M. Mollel (Little, Brown and Company, 1992)

Questions

1. Why was the small Bat chosen to bring rain to his land?
2. What reasons did the Moon, Stars, Clouds, and Winds give for not helping the small Bat?
3. What promise did the small Bat make to the Sun in return for providing rain?
4. What prevented the small Bat from keeping his promise to the Sun and how did his failure to keep his promise change his life?
5. How does the legend *A Promise to the Sun* offer a cultural explanation as to why bats must live in darkness?

Outcomes

1. To appreciate an African legend and how it is used to explain specific features of the natural world
2. To investigate and analyze how legends provide insight into different world cultures.

Materials

- "Promising the Sun: An African Legend" worksheet
- pencil
- colored pencils or crayons

Discussion

The African legend *A Promise to the Sun* is a powerful story about a bat who sacrifices his way of life for the good of his cousins, the birds. Like the birds he saves, the small bat has wings. However, his mouselike body and membranous wings separate him from his beaked and feathered friends. The story of his search for rain, and his promise to the sun in return for rain, offer a cultural explanation as to why bats must live in darkness rather than light.

Like most legends, *A Promise to the Sun* begins with a problem (a severe drought). Encourage students to discuss the problem and the events that followed the decision to send the small Bat out to search for rain. Ask what resolutions resulted from the small Bat's encounters with the Sun.

Using the "Promising the Sun: An African Legend" worksheet, ask students to illustrate the sequence of the story beginning with its problem, and then showing its events and the resolution. Culminate the activity by having students share how they would change this story to fit it into their own culture. (That is, who would they send to get rain if their land was being threatened by drought?)

Interdisciplinary Activities

Window Into African Culture

Introduction

Most legends tell more than just a story. They are often cultural expressions of the people who created them. Tololwa Mollel's tale of the bat's promise to the sun, for example, is a window to understanding her culture's need to explain the unknown. In this story, Mollell explains why bats live in darkness and why the sun hesitates before making its daily move below the horizon.

Like the Maasai of Africa, many cultures feel a need to describe the unknown elements of nature through the creation of myths and legends. These stories, passed on from generation to generation, provide valuable information for students studying world cultures.

Outcomes

1. To investigate and evaluate African culture through legend
2. To respect folklore as an important resource in the study of world cultures

Materials

• "Window into African Culture" worksheet

Procedure

1. There are many diverse cultures around the world. Begin the activity by asking students to define and discuss the concept of culture. Questions to be addressed should include:

   a. What important factors create a culture? (geography, climate, economy, religion, family organization, government, etc.)

   b. How do cultures maintain their distinctiveness?

   c. What role do legends play in cultural maintenance?

2. Encourage students to share myths, legends, or folktales from familiar cultures. How do these stories provide specific cultural information? Using the "Window into African Culture" worksheet, have students describe how Mollel's tale of the small Bat's promise to the Sun is a window to peer into African culture. Culminate the activity by having students share their cultural descriptions.

Extending the Theme

• Write a story that takes place in a bat cave.
• Create a cartoon strip depicting the small Bat's adventure with the Sun.

Creating a Legend

Introduction

Why is the sky so far away? Why do the stars shine? Why do zebras have stripes? These questions and many others have been answered in a variety of ways through the myths and legends of world cultures.

People from all cultures seem to have a need to explain the wonders and secrets of the universe in their own ways. Outsiders may challenge the local beliefs generated by these longstanding myths and legends, but they are often unsuccessful in changing the commitment people feel to folklore regarding the unknown.

Perhaps the resistance to change beliefs that were passed from generation to generation can also be viewed as a resiliency to maintain cultural identity. Myths and legends can only provide meaning to people who believe them. Without the belief, the myth or legend dies. Usually, the culture dies along with the beliefs that gave it life and made it unique.

Outcomes

1. To explore several world cultures through their legends
2. To create a legend that explains a specific feature of the natural world

Materials

• myths, legends, folktales from cultures around the world (use the World Cultures bibliography)
• "Creating a Legend" worksheet

Procedure

1. Select two or three myths, legends, or folktales from different cultures of the world. Introduce them to the class and discuss how folklore helps us understand diverse cultures.

2. Ask each student to bring in a myth, legend, or folktale that represents a specific world culture. The World Cultures bibliography will help guide them in their selections.

3. Design a classroom display using the folklore collected by you and your students. Take one or two selections from the display each day and share it as a class. Students might also enjoy having the display available to them during their free or quiet times.

4. Once students seem to understand the value of using folklore in the study of world cultures, ask them to think about creating their own myth, legend, or folktale. As a class, generate a list of possible natural features that would be suitable for explanation through folklore. Examples might include: why bears hibernate, why the sun rises and sets daily, why zebras have stripes, why the sky seems so far away, why the moon changes as it goes through its monthly cycle, and why elephants have trunks.

5. Have students write their story following the format provided on the "Creating a Legend" worksheet. Finished stories can be compiled into a class booklet and displayed with the other myths, legends, and folktales of cultures around the world.

Extending the Theme

• Create a "World Cultures Through Folklore" school bag that can be borrowed by students to take home and share with their parents.

• Write a "World Cultures Through Folklore" bibliography as a class project

Name: _____   Date: _____

Promising the Sun: An African Legend

Use the following statements to illustrate the sequence of the legend *A Promise to the Sun*.

1. Long ago, a severe drought hit the land of the birds.

2. The birds asked the small Bat to search for rain.

3. The small Bat went to the Moon, Stars, Clouds, and Winds but had no success. He finally went to the Sun.

4. The Sun agreed to provide rain in exchange for a promise.

5. Rain came and the birds were so busy with harvest celebrations, they did not help the small Bat keep his promise to the Sun.

6. The small Bat panicked and hid in a cave to avoid the Sun's anger. The small Bat had to stay there and learn to live in darkness.

1

2

3

4

5

6

Name: _____ **Date:** _____

Window into African Culture

Using the diagram of the window below, identify four features of the African culture that you learned by reading *A Promise to the Sun*.

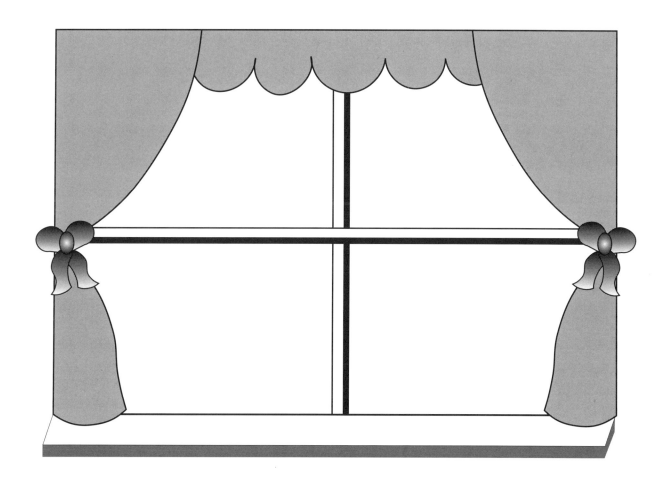

1. _____ 2. _____

3. _____ 4. _____

Name: _____ **Date:** _____

Creating A Legend

A Promise to the Sun explains why bats live in darkness. It also explains why the sun pauses before moving below the horizon. Create your own myth or legend explaining a natural occurrence. An example of this would be "Why do trees' leaves turn colors in autumn?" Use the format below to write your story.

Problem: _____

_____

_____

Event: _____

_____

_____

Event: _____

_____

_____

Resolution: _____

_____

_____

Celebrating Sunrise Around the World

Introduction

Each new day on the earth is greeted by a sunrise. As the sun makes its daily move from east to west, people around the world honor its presence in many different ways. Some honor it through prayers and blessings, others through traditional chants or songs. Regardless of the way the sun is honored, people from all regions of the world feel the need, in their own way, to respect and celebrate each new day.

The Way to Start a Day by Byrd Baylor offers wonderful insights into the multitude of ways people around the world commemorate the gift of each new sunrise. From the ancient pharaohs of Egypt to the modern pueblo cornfields of New Mexico, Baylor's verse is magical and inspirational.

Reading Activity

The Way to Start a Day

by Byrd Baylor (Aladdin Books, 1986)

Questions

1. Why is honoring the sun an important way to start a day?
2. What are several ways people honor a sunrise?
3. Why do some world cultures bring presents to the sun?
4. What is the author's message to all the earth's residents?
5. How is greeting the sun relevant to your daily lifestyle?

Outcomes

1. To recognize and appreciate the different ways people around the world honor the arrival of the sunrise
2. To record and chart sunrise and sunset over a two-week period
3. To write a narrative essay giving a personal explanation of how one should welcome and honor a new sunrise

Materials

- "Celebrating Sunrise Around the World" worksheet
- pencil

Discussion

The people of the sun temples in Peru chant to the sun to acknowledge its gift of a new day. In India, people gather by shrines with marigolds in their hands, while others bath in the holy Ganges River. High on a mesa ledge in Arizona, a baby is held up to the sun to be filled with the power of life that the sun brings to the earth. Each celebrates the omnipotence of the sun in his or her own way.

Discuss the different ways people around the world have traditionally honored the morning sun. Using the "Celebrating Sunrise Around the World" worksheet, have students record what people from these diverse world cultures do that is unique and special to them.

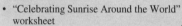

Interdisciplinary Activities

Welcoming the Sun

Introduction

Some people believe that there is a new sun born at dawn each day. Since its life is only for one day, the world must welcome it and make it a good day for the sun's one-day life.

Where do we begin to welcome the sun? The best place, it is said, is to look east, into the sky at dawn. There, like many other people around the world, we can offer our thoughts, prayers, and songs to a rising sun. Watching the sun rise, we will feel the hope that begins each new day.

Outcomes

1. To identify the best places to welcome the sun
2. To write a narrative essay describing a personal way to greet a sunrise and the start of a new day

Materials

- "Welcoming the Sun" worksheet

Procedure

1. Review the different ways the sun is welcomed throughout the world. Discuss why many ancient and contemporary cultures feel the need to honor the sunrise of each new day.

2. Have students generate a list of possible locations in their local area where they would like to go to watch a sunrise. What would they do to welcome the sun in each of these areas? Would they choose to go alone or with someone special? Why?

3. Distribute the "Welcoming the Sun" worksheet. Ask students to think about an unique way they might use to welcome the sun. They should describe what they would do and why they would do it.

4. Culminate the activity by having students share their stories as a class.

Extending the Theme

- Create a myth explaining why the sun rises and sets each day.
- Make up a dance routine to celebrate sunrise.

• • • • • • • • • • • • • •

Activity 2   Charting Sunrise and Sunset

Introduction

The sun is extremely important to life on the earth. By making its daily journey from sunrise to sunset, it provides many living things with the resources of heat, light, and rain that are so crucial to the survival on our planet. Plants, for example, need sunlight to grow. Animals need plants as a food source, and people need both plants and animals in order to maintain life. Without the sun, no living thing would exist on the earth.

Scientists believe that the sun has enough fuel to keep it burning another five billion years. If so, the sun will be providing the earth with sunrises and sunsets for many more generations. Earth's children should be encouraged to observe and respect this daily miracle; a miracle that gives them life with each new day.

Outcomes

1. To identify specific ways the sun is needed for the survival of the earth's living things
2. To chart the sunrises and sunsets over a period of two weeks and to determine the pattern that sunrises and sunsets follow over that time

Materials

- "Charting Sunrises and Sunsets" worksheet
- newspaper with sunrise and sunset times for your local area

Procedure

1. Discuss the importance of daily sunrises and sunsets for living things on the earth (heat, light, rain). Encourage students to think about what might happen when the sun's fuel runs out.

2. Introduce students to the section of a daily newspaper that tells the sunrise and sunset times for their local area. Ask them to discuss some of the information they might gain by recording sunrises and sunsets over a two-week period.

3. Provide each student with the "Charting Sunrises and Sunsets" worksheet. Using daily newspapers, have them record the dates, sunrise, and sunset times over a two-week period.

4. Culminate this activity by asking students to determine the sunrise and sunset pattern during the recorded period. They can answer this question on the same worksheet they used to chart their data.

Extending the Theme

- Research ancient theories about the sun by studying early scientists (Ptolemy, Copernicus, Galileo, Kepler, and Newton).
- Investigate solar energy and how it is being used today

Name: _____   **Date:** _____

Celebrating Sunrise Around the World

How do the following areas of the world celebrate sunrise?

Peru _____

Mexico _____

African Congo _____

China _____

Egypt _____

Japan _____

India _____

Pueblos of Arizona _____

Welcoming the Sun

Create a special poem, chant, song, or activity you would like to use to greet the sun. Describe where and how you would use your gift to welcome the sun.

Name: _____ Date: _____

Charting Sunrises and Sunsets

Chart the dates and times of sunrises and sunsets for two weeks.

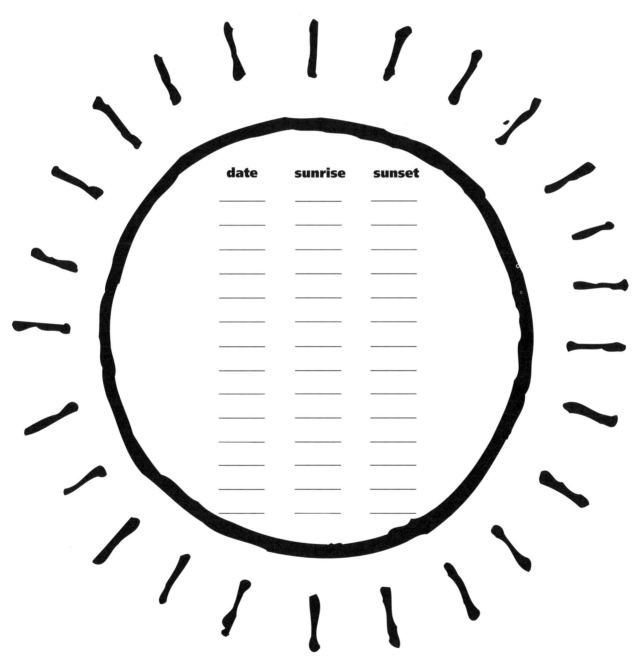

date	sunrise	sunset
_____	_____	_____
_____	_____	_____
_____	_____	_____
_____	_____	_____
_____	_____	_____
_____	_____	_____
_____	_____	_____
_____	_____	_____
_____	_____	_____
_____	_____	_____
_____	_____	_____
_____	_____	_____
_____	_____	_____
_____	_____	_____

Question: What pattern do sunrises and sunsets follow?

Response: _____

Introduction

The wind that gently blows in your window on a summer night is the same wind that ripples quiet waters, spins the arms of windmills, whistles over rocky slopes, and drives the thunder and lighting of a summer storm over pasture lands.

No one can see the wind that is a part of our daily lives, but we can feel its many different speeds. Light winds can bring comfort on a hot summer day, while the swirling winds of a tornado can bring death and destruction to anyone or anything in its pathway.

In her book *The Same Wind*, Bette Killion explores the ways people around the world experience the same wind. This book motivates students to learn more about the wind—its impact on their daily lives.

Reading Activity

The Same Wind

by Bette Killion (Laura Geringer Book; Imprint of HarperCollins, 1992)

Questions

1. What prompted the author to write this book?
2. How does the author relate the wind to the different seasons of the year?
3. How does the author use the wind to describe diverse landscapes?
4. Where were the windmills described by the author, and how do you think windmills got their name?
5. How does the wind influence your daily life?

Outcomes

1. To study the wind and its impact on our everyday lives
2. To aesthetically appreciate the wind in its variety of forms

Materials

- a dictionary
- "World Winds" worksheet
- pencil

Discussion

The wind can be described in many ways, and Killion provides her readers with a variety of examples: the wind that sweeps over forests, the wind that stirs the tumbleweed into activity, and the wind that swirls over the vast flatlands leaving devastation in its wake.

Ask students to generate a class list of the various types of wind they have experienced. Discuss how some forms of wind are helpful while others are harmful.

Review what an adjective is and how adjectives can be used in describing the types of wind on your class list.

Using the "World Winds" worksheet, have students write down four adjectives describing the wind during the following times: during a storm, during winter, during summer, over the water, and at night. Culminate the activity by having students share the adjectives they used as a class.

Interdisciplinary Activities

Activity 1   Wind Patterns Around the World

Introduction

Air is in constant movement around the earth. As the air moves, wind patterns are created by the differences in temperature and by the earth's spinning motion. The warm air around the equator, for example, rises very quickly and spreads north and south, ultimately falling back to earth in the two areas known as the horse latitudes. The trade winds, blown from the horse winds, return to the equator. The westerlies, also coming from the horse winds, eventually meet the cold winds of the poles where they become polar easterlies.

Since winds tend to come from the same direction, most regions of the world experience similar weather patterns over a long period of time (climate). Learning about the different types of wind and their circulation patterns is crucial to understanding different climates around the world.

Outcomes

1. To identify the earth's wind patterns and the direction the wind moves to create these patterns
2. To relate the movement of the earth's wind to the different types of climate found around the world

Materials

- "Wind Patterns Around the World" worksheet
- a reference book that illustrates the earth's wind patterns (a good example would be *Wind: Causes and Effects* by Philip Steele. Franklin Watts, 1991)

Procedure

1. Using an illustration of the earth's wind patterns, discuss the types of wind patterns and the direction they move from the equator to the polar regions of our planet.

2. Define the terms climate and prevailing wind. Encourage students to critically think about how the wind influences different climates around the world, and why it is important to know the wind's patterns to understand world climates.

3. Using the "Wind Patterns Around the World" worksheet, ask students to identify and label on the global outline each wind pattern and the direction it moves. You might want to display a completed illustration of the world's wind patterns to guide students through this activity.

Extending Activities

- Find out what the prevailing wind is for your geographical area by observing and recording the wind's direction during several specific times each day (morning, afternoon, evening) for a period of one or two weeks. Determine the wind's direction at the same location each day. Design a bar graph that illustrates the collected data.

- Explore how wind and water work together to create the process of erosion.

• • • • • • • • • • • • • •

Activity 2 Wind and Weather

Introduction

The faster the air moves, the stronger the wind blows. Sir Francis Beaufort, a British admiral, worked out a scale for the wind's intensity in 1805. This scale was originally used at sea, but has since been adapted for use on land.

According to the Beaufort scale, a "calm" wind moves at the force of less than 1 mph, a "gentle" breeze moves at approximately 8–12 mph, and a "strong" gale moves at speeds of 47–54 mph. Winds with a force of 73 mph or greater (identified as Force 12 on the Beaufort scale) are considered hurricanes. Tornadoes produce the highest winds with speeds ranging from 100 to 300 mph.

Wind force often determines specific climatic features for distinct regions of the world. Sea breezes, hurricanes, dust devils, wind chill, and tornadoes all reflect the intensity of the wind's speed in relation to weather. Learning about the Beaufort scale and its utility in defining specific climatic patterns will allow children to understand the special connection between the wind and the weather.

Outcomes

1. To use the Beaufort scale to investigate wind patterns in relation to speed, force, and type of wind
2. To relate the Beaufort scale to specific weather patterns found around the world

Materials

- a reference book which illustrates the Beaufort scale (*Wind: Causes and Effects* by Philip Steele offers a good illustration as well as an explanation)
- "Wind and Weather" worksheet

Procedure

1. Discuss how the air's movement influences wind patterns. Illustrate the Beaufort scale and ask students to relate the force and speed of the wind with its classified type. You might also want students to discuss how different types of wind affect specific features of our landscape.

2. Using the "Wind and Weather" worksheet, have students describe each wind pattern with the weather it produces. Examples of wind patterns include sea breezes, hurricanes, tornadoes, dust devils, and wind chill. The causes and effects of each type of wind should be in the description. You might want to culminate this activity by asking students to illustrate a landscape reflective of a specific wind type.

Extending the Theme

- Explore weather superstitions and how people use them to explain the weather.
- Examples:
    1. "If the cows are lying down, it's going to rain soon."
    2. "If it snows on Christmas day, Easter will be green."
    3. "If you sleep with a flower under your pillow, the weather will be fair the next day."
    4. "Sit in the middle of a room and hold a glass of water in your hand, and you will not be struck by lightning during a storm."

    (*The Study of American Folklore* by Jan Harold Brunvand).

- Read or watch the film *The Wizard of Oz.* Have students write their own version of the story.

From *Discovering World Cultures Through Literature* published by GoodYearBooks. Copyright © 1995 Gerry Edwards.

World Winds

Use four adjectives to describe the different types of wind as associated with each of the following landscape scenes.

Storm Winds

1. _____   3. _____

2. _____   4. _____

Winter Winds

1. _____   3. _____

2. _____   4. _____

Summer Winds

1. _____   3. _____

2. _____   4. _____

Winds over the Water

1. _____   3. _____

2. _____   4. _____

Night Winds

1. _____   3. _____

2. _____   4. _____

Name: _____ Date: _____

Wind Patterns Around the World

Plot the following world wind patterns on the global outline below and indicate the direction each wind travels.

Polar Easterlies

North Westerlies

South Westerlies

Doldrums

Horse Latitudes

Southeast Trades

Northeast Trades

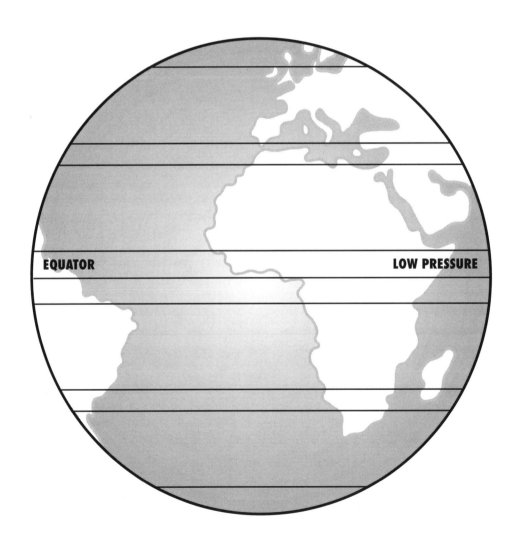

EQUATOR   LOW PRESSURE

Name: _____ Date: _____

Wind and Weather

Describe the following wind types with the weather each produces.

Sea Breezes: _____

_____

Hurricanes: _____

_____

Dust Devils: _____

_____

Chinook: _____

_____

Mistral: _____

_____

Sirocco: _____

_____

Tornadoes: _____

_____

Introduction

Try to imagine a world without water. Is it impossible? When we begin to think about what such a world would be like, we realize how much all living things depend on the earth's water. Why, then, do we waste it and pollute it?

Since we cannot live without water, we must learn all we can about it and place a priority on its conservation. By protecting the world's water, we protect our future.

Reading Activity

Water Up, Water Down: The Hydrologic Cycle

by Sally M. Walker (Carolrhoda Books, 1992)

Questions

1. What are the three forms of water?
2. What processes are part of the hydrologic cycle?
3. How do world cultures use water resources?
4. What is acid rain?
5. Why is conservation of the world's water supply so important to maintaining world cultures?

Outcomes

1. To learn about the way water moves, and the impact that movement has on our daily lives
2. To realize the importance of making water conservation a priority

Materials

- "Watering the World" worksheet
- pencil

Discussion

Water is made up of molecules. A water molecule is made up of two hydrogen atoms and one oxygen atom. The form water takes depends on the arrangement of the water molecules. When the molecules are closely bound, water takes the form of a solid (ice). When the molecules are looser, water becomes a liquid. Water vapor is created when the molecules move very freely, putting no restrictions on size or shape.

Water is constantly moving between the earth's surface and its atmosphere in a repeated pattern known as the hydrologic cycle. Humans depend on this cycle for many of their daily needs. Any threat to the continuation of the water cycle is a threat to human survival.

Have students think about the different ways people use the earth's water cycle in their daily lives. Using the "Watering the World" worksheet, ask students to identify and describe how world cultures use the earth's water in specific areas (shelter, food, recreation, transportation, clothing, and religious rituals and beliefs). This activity can be culminated by having students create a class list to show ways world cultures depend on water.

Interdisciplinary Activities

Activity 1   The Hydrologic Cycle

Introduction

Oceans provide 97% of the world's water, glaciers provide 2%, and the remaining 1% comes from water found on top of and underneath the earth's surface and in the atmosphere.

As water is heated by the sun, it turns into vapor and then is returned to the air. (evaporation). When the water vapor cools, it condenses and then turns back into a liquid. It then falls to the ground in the form of rain, hail, or snow. This water cycle is known as the hydrologic cycle.

This activity will require students to know the terms associated with the hydrologic cycle and to illustrate this cycle using those terms.

Outcomes

1. To define and describe the vocabulary pertinent to the hydrologic cycle
2. To illustrate and label the processes and pattern of the water cycle

Materials

- dictionaries
- illustrations of the water cycle
- "The Hydrologic Cycle" worksheet

Procedure

1. Introduce an illustration of the hydrologic cycle (Walker's illustration is on page 41). Review the pattern that water follows as it is processed from the earth's surface to the atmosphere and back again to the earth's surface.

2. Divide students into groups of two. Provide each student with "The Hydrologic Cycle" worksheet and each group with a dictionary. Ask students to define the vocabulary listed, and to use that vocabulary in drawing an illustration that depicts the hydrologic cycle.

Extending the Theme

- Rainbows are produced by millions of tiny raindrops refracting and reflecting light. Create your own rainbow by using a garden hose and standing with your back to the sun. Adjust the spray to a fine mist and watch a rainbow come to life!

- It is said that no two snowflakes are alike. Design your own snowflakes and display them in the classroom or hallway.

• • • • • • • • • • • • • •

Activity 2   Water Conservation

Introduction

Conserving the earth's water supply should concern all cultures of the world. Dangerous chemicals carelessly thrown away, such as chemical fertilizers and pesticides that are used to better our crops and beautify our lawns, are contaminating the water supply.

Earth's water supply will always remain the same. It is up to us to make sure that our water is protected. People can prevent water pollution. We can begin by being more careful about the way we store and use dangerous chemicals and waste materials. We can keep our waters clean and safe for all people by simply making it a priority every day.

Outcomes

1. To identify and recognize the chemicals and waste materials threatening earth's water supply
2. To critically think about ways people can stop water pollution

Materials

- "Water Conservation" worksheet

Procedure

1. Begin by defining the word conservation and discussing how it applies to the earth's water supply. Discuss the different water sources and how each is being polluted (earth's surface, beneath the surface, and atmosphere).

2. Have each student bring in an article or book on water pollution or conservation. Ask students to tell the class what they learned by reading the article or book, and what information they feel is important to pass on to others.

3. Culminate the activity by assigning the "Water Conservation" worksheet.

Extending the Theme

- Write a description of what the world would be like without water. Illustrate the description.

- Watch how vapor condenses by filling a drinking glass with cold water. Add ice cubes and observe how the vapor in the warm air causes water to condense on the outside of the glass.

Watering the World

Describe how world cultures depend on the earth's water supply in the following areas:

Shelter:

Food:

Recreation:

Transportation:

Clothing:

Customs/Traditions/Holidays:

The Hydrologic Cycle

Define the following terms and illustrate the hydrologic cycle using those terms.

Evaporation: _____

Transpiration: _____

Groundwater: _____

Vapor: _____

Precipitation: _____

Illustration

Name: _____ **Date:** _____

Water Conservation

Question: What are the causes of water pollution around the world?

Response: _____

_____

_____

_____

_____

Question: How can people help to conserve the earth's water supply?

Response: _____

_____

_____

_____

_____

Drylongso and the Land Without Water

Introduction

Many people around the world endure long periods of time without rain. The drought scorches their lands and they worry whether they can survive.

Virginia Hamilton has written a wonderful story about how one African American family strove to save their crops from a severe drought west of the Mississippi River during the 1970s. It is a story about a family working together to save the land they love so dearly. The story is about hope and fate that came to this family in the form of a boy named Drylongso.

Reading Activity

Drylongso

by Virginia Hamilton (Harcourt Brace Jovanovich, 1992)

Questions

1. How did Drylongso come into the lives of the small African American family who lived west of the Mississippi?
2. What was the family's initial reaction to Drylongso?
3. How did Drylongso help save Lindy's family from the drought?
4. How was Drylongso different from other children his age?
5. Why does the author portray Drylongso as a somewhat mythical folk hero?

Outcomes

1. To gain insight and understanding into how land with out water can be devastating
2. To analyze why people create folk heroes in times of struggle and hardship

Materials

- "Drylongso: Character Analysis" worksheet
- pencil

Discussion

After three years of living with little rain, Lindy and her family continue to work hard trying to save their crops from being destroyed by the drought. While tending the land with her father, Lindy notices a massive wall of dust coming their way. Running ahead of the dust storm is a boy named Drylongso. Lindy's family shelters Drylongso, and in return he finds a water supply to secure the growth of their newly planted crops.

The characters created by Virginia Hamilton are plain, hardworking people who deeply care about each other and the land they are trying to save. Have students discuss the story and how Hamilton's characters helped each other to survive the dust storm and the drought. Using the "Drylongso: Character Analysis" worksheet, ask students to record how each character showed concern for the others during a time of crisis.

You might want to culminate this activity by asking each student to do a character analysis of their own family. Have them explain how each family member helped the others to solve a difficult problem or to make a difficult decision.

Interdisciplinary Activities

Activity 1 Drylongso: A Cultural Hero

Introduction

Severe drought generally occurs in the United States at regular intervals of twenty years. *Drylongso,* a term describing the nature of a drought, was originally passed down by generations of African Americans living during the Plantation Era.

People living during the hard times of a drought, like most people confronting difficult economic times, look to their culture's heroes. These heroes provide them with the strength to face their hardships and with a hope that the future will be brighter.

Hamilton made Drylongso a cultural hero by endowing him with mythical qualities that allowed him to save Lindy and her family from the drought's afflictions. The magical properties of a divining rod permitted Drylongso to determine the destiny of a drought-ridden people.

Outcomes

1. To analyze Drylongso as a cultural hero
2. To compare and contrast two cultural heroes

Materials

- "Comparing Two Cultural Heroes" worksheet

Procedure

1. Define the term *cultural hero.* Discuss how Drylongso was seen as a hero in the lives of Lindy and her family. What qualities did he possess that made him appear mythical? How do some of Drylongso's qualities compare with the qualities of other culturally defined heroes (George Washington, Abraham Lincoln, Davy Crockett, Martin Luther King, Eleanor Roosevelt, Harriet Tubman, etc.).

2. Have students generate a class list of people they would identify as cultural heroes. Ask them to choose two people on the list and compare how they are alike and different. Use the Venn diagram on the "Comparing Two Cultural Heroes" work sheet to help students complete this assignment. Share the completed comparisons as a class.

Extending the Theme

- Create cultural hero puzzles by gathering old photographs or illustrations, attaching them to cardboard, and cutting out zig-zag shapes to make each puzzle unique.

- List ten vocabulary words that would be used to define or describe a drought. Have students define each word and use it in a sentence.

• • • • • • • • • • • • • •

Activity 2   Women Are Cultural Heroes Too!

Introduction

Why is it that when we think of heroes, many of us think only about heroes who are men?

Many women of the past have heroic tales to tell. However, their voices have often gone unheard because of the heroic deeds of their fathers, brothers, and sons in a society where women were to stay quietly in the background.

It is time for these women to share their heroic tales. By sharing their stories, people of the world will better understand that women are as brave and powerful as men. Children, in particular, must realize that heroism is not related to gender.

Heroines such as Bess Call, Annie Christmas, Pale-Faced Lightning, Hiiaka, and many others are the equals to such heroes as Davy Crockett, Johnny Appleseed, and Paul Bunyan. Once you hear these women's stories, you will not forget them.

Outcomes

1. To read and examine several heroic tales of American women in myth and legend
2. To compare and contrast the heroic tales of American women with those of American men

Materials

- myths, legends, and tall tales that depict women as heroes (*Cut from the Same Cloth* by Robert D. San Souci and Brian Pinkney, Philomel Books, 1993, is an excellent reference)
- "Women Are Cultural Heroes Too!" worksheet

Procedure

1. Choose an American woman you consider to be a cultural heroine and introduce her to the class by sharing her background or a story that tells why she is considered a woman of power and courage. (You might want to choose a myth, legend, or tall tale from *Cut from the Same Cloth* and read it to the class.)

2. As a class, try to develop a list of other women who could be considered cultural heroes. Discuss the background of these women and how they compare to familiar male heroes.

3. Provide students with the "Women Are Cultural Heroes Too!" worksheet. Ask each student to choose three heroic women and research the activities that made them cultural heroes. Students can record the information on the worksheet. They should include the folk hero's name, her background, and a description of her heroic activities.

4. As a culminating activity, ask students to discuss and share their heroines. They might wish to read a myth or legend about their heroine or they can use their worksheet to describe her famous feats.

Extending the Theme

- Play a game called "Guess the Hero." Each student uses the three heroines they researched and writes their names on an index card with three clues to identify their heroine. Divide the class into two groups and have each group try to guess the other group's heroine. If they guess it on the first clue, its worth three points; second clue, two points; and third clue, one point. The group with the most points wins.

- List ten complaints you might hear from people experiencing a drought.

Name: _____ Date: _____

Drylongso: Character Analysis

How do the characters in the story help each other during the drought of 1975?

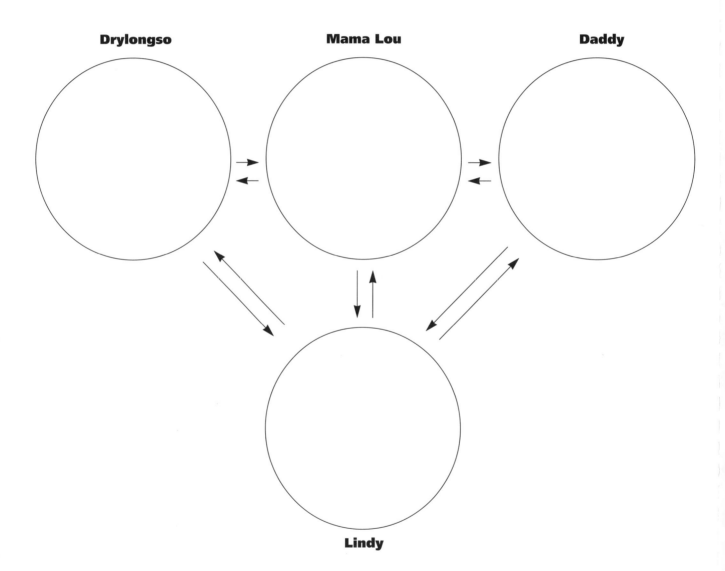

Name: _____   **Date:** _____

Comparing Two Cultural Heroes

Choose two cultural heroes and record their similarities and differences on the Venn diagram.

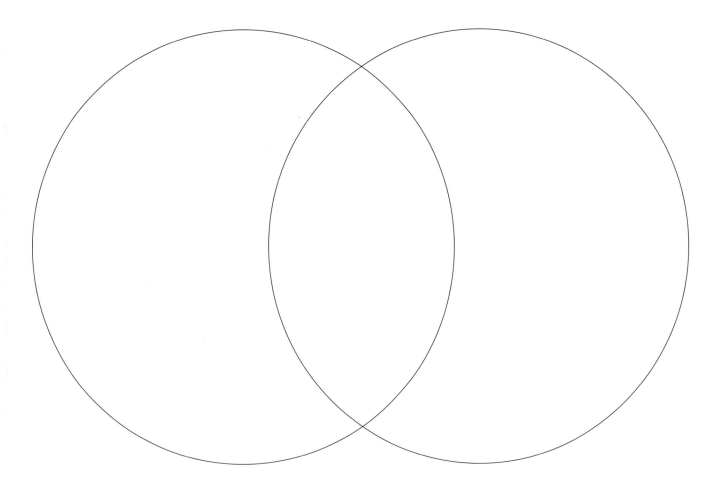

Name: _____   Date: _____

Women Are Cultural Heroes Too!

Choose three women you consider cultural heroines. Identify who they are and describe their background and the activities that made them heroines.

Folk Heroine:

Background:

Description of Heroic Activities:

Folk Heroine:

Background:

Description of Heroic Activities:

Folk Heroine:

Background:

Description of Heroic Activities:

Reading Activity

On the Day You Were Born

by Debra Frasier (Harcourt Brace Jovanovich, 1991)

Introduction

According to Debra Frasier's book, *On the Day You Were Born,* all the elements of the earth played a part in making the world a welcome place for your survival. Her story is a reflection of her sensitivity and reverence for the natural world. Her text and illustrations integrate her respect for nature by allowing us to see how the earth takes care of each of its children.

It is crucial that children learn how to take care of their planet so it may continue to welcome new life.

Questions

1. According to the story, how does the news of each new birth migrate around the world?
2. How do the sun, the moon, and the stars help to welcome you into the world?
3. What does gravity do to secure your position on the earth?
4. Why do people sing when new life is given to the world?
5. How can you help the earth to continue greeting each new child that is born around the world?

Outcomes

1. To explore how the earth welcomes the birth of each of its children
2. To appreciate and develop a respect for taking care of the earth

Materials

- "The Earth Welcomes You" worksheet
- pencil

Discussion

The earth works in mysterious ways. According to the story, one of the most mysterious things about the earth is its ability to bring life into the world. Discuss how the stars, the sun, the moon, and the people of the earth play a role in greeting each new life. Why is it important for people to respect the role they play in the coming of each new arrival?

Using "The Earth Welcomes You" worksheet, ask students to recall how the earth's elements welcomed them on the day they were born.

Culminate the activity by having students share their responses, and discuss how they can help secure the earth's gift of life to children not yet born.

Interdisciplinary Activities

Activity 1 The World Working Together

Introduction

People around the world must work together to ensure the earth's future. Children should become more aware of and knowledgeable about the earth's natural elements. They should pay greater attention to how these elements work together, and they should learn to appreciate the important role they play in sustaining life on the earth.

Frasier gives very clear and concise descriptions of the natural elements that make up the earth. By investigating the duties of each natural element, children will be able to see how the parts work together to create the earth.

Outcomes

1. To identify the earth's elements and the role each plays to support life on the earth
2. To appreciate the different ways all of the earth's elements work together to maintain life as we know it

Materials

- "The World Working Together" worksheet

Procedure

1. Generate a class list of the earth's elements and ask students to share what they know about each element. The following elements should be included on your list: animals, plants, gravity, sun, moon, stars, tides, air, and rain. Use Frasier's descriptions of these elements to expand class discussion (located at the back of the book under the section "More About the World around You").

2. Ask students to look at Frasier's illustrations and tell how each illustration reflects the job of a particular element.

3. Provide each student with the "The World Working Together" worksheet. Have each student list two ways each of the outlined elements works to support life on the earth.

Extending the Theme

- Describe three ways you can help secure the earth's future.

- Illustrate a rescue mission to save the earth.

• • • • • • • • • • • • • •

Activity 2   I Hear the World Singing

Introduction

Music plays an important role in understanding different cultures around the world. Although the style of music may vary, the themes are often shared by most world cultures. People around the world sing songs to express their common emotions, religious beliefs, and historical past, as well as their hopes and dreams for the future.

As children around the world learn more about each other, it is important to highlight activities that unite people of all cultures, in spirit and in purpose. Unifying our world through song is an excellent way to begin this bonding process.

Outcomes

1. To become aware of how music can be instrumental to a better understanding of world cultures
2. To write the lyrics for a song that could be sung around the world to unify all its people

Materials

- different types of world music
- "I Hear the World Singing" worksheet

Procedure

1. Choose a variety of music representing different world cultures (African, Native American, Latin American, European, American, etc.). Listen to the different types of music as a class and discuss the various ways music is used by world cultures to bring meaning and purpose to everyday life.

2. Have students list or identify songs from their own culture that address the themes of world unity and peace. Go through the lyrics of these songs and discuss how the words exemplify global unity.

3. Using the "I Hear the World Singing" worksheet, have students write the lyrics for a unifying song. Have students take the music from one of their favorite songs and parody it using the lyrics they created.

4. Culminate the activity by asking students to volunteer to sing their songs for their classmates.

Extending the Theme

- Using the songs generated by the class, plan a traveling concert for the benefit of global unity and peace.

- Write a thank-you note to "Mother Earth" for welcoming you into the world on the day you were born.

Name: _____ Date: _____

The Earth Welcomes You

How did the following elements of the earth greet
you on the day you were born?

Animals: _____

Gravity: _____

Sun: _____

Moon: _____

Stars: _____

Waves: _____

Clouds: _____

Trees: _____

People: _____

Illustrate one of the above elements welcoming you on the day you were born.

The World Working Together

Using the outline below, list two ways each of the earth's elements greet the birth of each new child.

Migrating Animals

1. _____

2. _____

Sun

1. _____

2. _____

Moon

1. _____

2. _____

People

1. _____

2. _____

Gravity

1. _____

2. _____

Stars

1. _____

2. _____

Air

1. _____

2. _____

Rain

1. _____

2. _____

Trees

1. _____

2 _____

Name: _____ **Date:** _____

I Hear the World Singing

Write the lyrics for a song that could be sung around the world to promote global unity and peace.

While Alice sat on her grandfather's lap listening to stories of faraway places, she dreamed of going to those faraway places herself. Grandfather was pleased, but he told Alice that there was one very important thing she must do in her life. She must do something to make the world more beautiful.

What would the world be like if we all followed Grandfather's advice to Alice? Barbara Cooney, author and illustrator of *Miss Rumphius,* has written a simple and heartwarming story about a girl who seeks to follow her grandfather's advice. Her journey to find the one thing she can do to make the world more beautiful is a story children and adults can treasure.

Reading Activity

Miss Rumphius

by Barbara Cooney (Viking, 1982)

Questions

1. What two dreams did Miss Rumphius have as a child?
2. What did Alice's grandfather tell her she must do in her life?
3. What faraway places did Miss Rumphius visit?
4. What did Miss Rumphius do to make the world more beautiful?
5. How would you like to make the world more beautiful?

Outcomes

1. To empathize with the desire Miss Rumphius has to do something to make the world more beautiful
2. To appreciate and adopt a universal belief that the world begins with the beauty inside each one of us

Materials

- "Miss Rumphius" worksheet
- pencil

Discussion

When Miss Rumphius was grown, she set out to do the three things she promised her grandfather she would do. While a young lady, she visited a tropical island, climbed snow-covered mountains, and explored the land of lotus-eaters on a camel's back. When she grew older, she found her place by the sea. Finally, after much searching, she discovered her way of making the world more beautiful. The blue, purple, and rose-colored flowers she spread along the countryside bloomed into magnificently elegant lupines. Miss Rumphius had now fulfilled her three childhood dreams.

Ask students to discuss the dreams Miss Rumphius wanted to fulfill in her lifetime. Encourage students to share the dreams they have for their future and how they think they can begin to fulfill their dreams. Using the "Miss Rumphius" worksheet, have students describe what Miss Rumphius did to make her dreams come true.

Interdisciplinary Activities

Activity 1   Faraway Places

Introduction

We have all had a desire to visit a faraway place and share in a culture different from our own. Miss Rumphius also dreamed of faraway places, and those dreams led her to new lands and new experiences.

Teaching children to appreciate and respect the diversity of human behavior is one of the greatest gifts we can give to them. It allows them to see beyond themselves and to accept the many different ways people around the world organize their lives. Learning to respect other world cultures is the first step toward global peace and survival.

Outcomes

1. To celebrate the belief that all cultures should be respected
2. To adopt a global perspective that encourages each and every member of the earth to respect and learn from each other

Materials

- reference materials about faraway places
- "Faraway Places" worksheet

Procedure

1. Have students discuss the faraway places Miss Rumphius visited. Encourage students to share some of the faraway places they have visited and how these places were similar to and different than their community.

2. Introduce several reference books about countries and cultures distant to your local region. Ask students to browse through the books and write down several places they might like to visit.

3. Have students use the "Faraway Places" worksheet to record the places they would like to visit in each of the listed countries. Culminate the activity by having students share why they chose the places they did.

Extending the Theme

- Write a biography of Miss Rumphius.
- Use photographs and illustrations to design a travel poster of your favorite place in the world.

• • • • • • • • • • • • • • •

Activity 2   Making the World More Beautiful

Introduction

Keeping with her grandfather's wishes, Miss Rumphius found her way of making the world more beautiful. As her lupines graced the countryside of her house by the sea, people near and far appreciated the beauty she had given to their homeland.

Following in the spirit of Miss Rumphius, we can all make the world more beautiful. All we have to do is want to. It sounds simple, but facing cynical adults is a major obstacle to convincing children they can truly make a difference. We must begin by believing it ourselves.

Outcomes

1. To encourage students to believe that they can make a difference in today's world and in the future
2. To have students choose a favorite place and then create a way they can make it more beautiful

Materials

- "Making the World More Beautiful" worksheet

Procedure

1. Discuss how Miss Rumphius went about her task of making the world more beautiful. What was the reaction of those living around her? How did people react when they saw the lupines blossoming all over the countryside?

2. Encourage students to share their feelings about the commitment Miss Rumphius felt in fulfilling her grandfather's wish. Ask them to think about a favorite place they would like to make more beautiful. Using the "Making the World More Beautiful" worksheet, ask students to describe their favorite place, what they would do to make it more beautiful, and how would they accomplish it. Have students illustrate their favorite place "before" and "after" their efforts to make it more beautiful.

3. Culminate the activity by having students share their completed assignments.

Extending the Theme

- List ten ways you can make your neighborhood more beautiful.
- You have just completed a book titled *Making the World More Beautiful*. Design a cover for your book.

Name: _____   **Date:** _____

Miss Rumphius

Sitting upon her grandfather's knee, young Alice had three dreams for the future. The first one was to travel to faraway places, the second was to live by the sea when she got older, and the third was to do something to make the world more beautiful. Describe what she did as each of her dreams came true.

Visits to Faraway Places

Live by the Sea When Older

Do Something to Make the World More Beautiful

Name: _____ **Date:** _____

Faraway Places

If you could travel to the following places, what would you most want to see during your visit?

Japan

China

Alaska

Mexico

Germany

Russia

Australia

Peru

New Zealand

Name: _____ **Date:** _____

Making the World More Beautiful

Choose a favorite place in the world. Describe one way you could make it more beautiful and how you would do it.

Illustrate the "before" and "after" of your favorite place.

Introduction

Somewhere tomorrow—
Will a sea otter float on
its back for lunch? Will
a spotted skunk be doing
a handstand?

Somewhere today these
strange and wonderful
animal behaviors are
taking place. Bert
Kitchen captures their
ritualistic behaviors of
play, work, and
courtship with
harmonious words and
illustrations.

The question for today is
whether or not these
marvelous animals will
be able to endure all the
environmental changes
threatening their
survival. Will they be
part of our world
tomorrow?

It is our responsibility to
teach our children about
the struggles many
members of our animal
kingdom are facing, and
together devise ways to
help these animals
survive.

Reading Activity

Somewhere Today

by Bert Kitchen (Candlewick Press, 1992)

Questions

1. How does the chameleon reach out for food?
2. Why do bald eagles plummet through the sky with their talons locked?
3. Why did the author call this book *Somewhere Today?*
4. How do the animals' rituals of work and play relate to your life?
5. What other animals not included in Kitchen's book perform interesting and ritualistic behaviors?

Outcomes

1. To develop an awareness and respect for all the animals of the world, particularly endangered animals
2. To discuss and formulate specific ways people of the world can help endangered animals

Materials

- "Somewhere Today" worksheet
- pencil

Discussion

Kitchen describes and illustrates many fascinating behaviors of various animals around the world. These ritualistic behaviors are taking place daily.

As a class, encourage students to recall some of the animals and their ritualistic behaviors portrayed by Kitchen in his book. Discuss how some of these animals are endangered, why they are endangered, and how we can help in securing their survival.

Using the "Somewhere Today" worksheet, have students describe what the listed animals are doing "somewhere today" and why.

Interdisciplinary Activities

| Activity 1 | The Endangered Animals of Our World Environments |

Introduction

The rain forests, grasslands, deserts, mountains, and polar regions of the world are continually being threatened by human intervention. Many of the animals inhabiting these regions are becoming endangered. What can we do, as parents and educators, to encourage our children to become involved in global issues relating to the protection of our world environments?

The first step we must take is to make our children aware that preserving world environments has a direct, positive impact on the preservation of world cultures. We hope that as greater numbers of children understand the relationship between environment and culture, they will begin to realize that to save the natural resources of our world environments is, in essence, to save themselves.

Outcomes

1. To identify endangered species of specific world environments
2. To critically evaluate the interdependent relationship between world environments and world cultures

Materials

• references on endangered species of the world (refer to specific bibliographies)
• "The Endangered Animals of Our World Environments" worksheet

Procedure

1. Encourage students to identify specific world environments that they have studied. Discuss each environment in relation to its endangered wildlife. Have students record the endangered animals of each environment by using "The Endangered Animals of Our World Environments" worksheet.

2. Divide students into six cooperative groups. Assign each group a specific world region to research. Ask them to identify several different kinds of animals that are endangered in their group's region and tell why they are endangered. Have each group draw up a plan for saving the endangered animals of their region.

3. Culminate the activity by having each group share their findings and survival plan with their classmates.

Extending the Theme

• Design a classroom mural illustrating endangered animals around the world in their specific environments.

• Describe the world you would like to see "somewhere tomorrow."

• • • • • • • • • • • • • •

| Activity 2 | ## The Bald Eagle: A Symbol of America's Environmental Heritage

Introduction

The eagle has been a symbol of courage, strength, and power to many countries throughout the world. Native Americans felt the eagle possessed special powers, the ancient Assyrians honored the eagle as a god, and the Persian and Roman armies went into battle carrying banners that displayed an eagle's image.

The bald eagle was chosen by the United States as its national bird. Many Americans have used the eagle as an emblem standing for excellence. An eagle scout, for example, is the highest rank in the Boy Scouts of America. An "eagle" is also a terrific golf score. "The Eagle has landed," were the words Neil Armstrong spoke following the first moon landing.

Since eagles are so revered around the world, particularly in the United States, why are we allowing them to be endangered? This activity will focus on why eagles are endangered and how different organizations are fighting for their survival.

Outcomes

1. To identify the reasons why eagles are endangered animals
2. To appreciate the honored position the eagle has held in American tradition and to discuss how people can be influential in saving this spectacular bird

Materials

• references that discuss and illustrate eagles in different types of environments (*Eagles* by Aubrey Lang, Little, 1990, is an excellent beginning)
• "Where Have All the Eagles Gone?" worksheet

Procedure

1. Choose several reference books about eagles and create a display area for your students. Introduce illustrations of eagles and discuss how for centuries eagles have been important to people throughout the world.

2. Encourage students to think about the different ways we are endangering the survival of eagle populations around the world (hunting, inadvertent poisoning, and pollution). Ask students to illustrate how pesticides enter the water supply and make their way into the eagle's food supply. Use the "Where Have All the Eagles Gone?" worksheet to help students complete this assignment (an illustration of this process can be found in Lang's book on eagles).

3. Culminate this activity by having students discuss the different organizations involved in helping eagles survive. Also, address any ideas they might have for helping eagles survive.

Extending the Theme

• Eagles are experts in soaring through the air. Why and how can they accomplish such splendorous feats?

• Write a narrative essay about how you are like an eagle.

Name: _____ Date: _____

Somewhere Today

What will the following animals be doing "somewhere today?" Why?

Sea Otter

Chameleon

Archerfish

Two Bald Eagles

Spotted Skunk

Dormouse

Western Grebes

Two Brown Hares

The Endangered Animals of Our World Environments

List two animals that are becoming endangered in the following world environments.

Rain Forests

1. _____

2. _____

Deserts

1. _____

2. _____

Grasslands

1. _____

2. _____

Mountains

1. _____

2. _____

Polar Regions

1. _____

2 _____

Seashores

1. _____

2. _____

Name: _____ Date: _____

Where Have All the Eagles Gone?

Illustrate the causes and effects of pesticide pollution as it moves from our water supply to the eagle's food supply. Begin by illustrating number one at the bottom of the page.

5. Eagles eat the water's poisoned fish.

4. Smaller fish are eaten by larger fish.

3. Small fish eat plankton.

2. Plankton in the water absorb the polluted water.

1. Humans introduce pesticides into the water, causing pollution.

Bibliography

Rain Forest Regions

Aldis, Rodney. *Ecology Watch: Rain Forests.* Dillon Press, 1991.

Baker, Lucy. *Life in the Rain Forests.* Franklin Watts, 1990.

Baker, Jeannie. *Where the Forest Meets the Sea.* Greenwillow, 1988.

Cochrane, Jennifer. *Green World: Trees of the Tropics.* Raintree Steck-Vaughn, 1990.

Cowcher, Helen. *Rain Forest.* Farrar Straus and Giroux, 1988.

Dorros, Arthur. *Rain Forest Secrets.* Scholastic, 1990.

George, Jean Craighead. *One Day in the Tropical Rain Forest.* HarperCollins, 1990.

George, Michael. *Rain Forest.* Creative Education, 1992.

Landau, Elaine. *Tropical Rain Forests Around the World.* Franklin Watts, 1990.

Langley, Andrew. *Jungles.* The Bookwright Press, 1987.

Mutel, Cornelia F., and Mary Rodgers. *Tropical Rain Forests: Our Endangered Planet.* Lerner Publications, 1991.

Rowland-Entwistle, Theodore. *Our World: Jungles and Rain Forests.* Silver Burdett, 1987.

Stone, Lynn. *Rain Forests.* Rourke Corp, 1989.

Warburton, Lois. *Rain Forests.* Lucent Books, 1991.

Williams, Lawrence. *Last Frontiers for Mankind: Jungles.* Marshall Cavendish, 1990.

Grassland Regions

Amsel, Sheri. *Habitats of the World: Grasslands.* Raintree Steck-Vaughn, 1992.

Anderson, Joan. *The American Family Farm.* Harcourt Brace Jovanovich, 1989.

Arnold, Caroline. *Tule Elk.* Carolrhoda Books, 1989.

Bash, Barbara. *Tree of Life: The World of the African Baobab.* Sierra Club Books– Little Brown and Company, 1989.

Berman, Ruth. *American Bison.* Carolrhoda Books, 1992.

Collinson, Alan. *Ecology Watch: Grasslands.* Dillon Press, 1992.

Greenaway, Theresa. *Green World: Grasses and Grains.* Raintree Steck-Vaughn, 1990.

Isadora, Rachel. *Over the Green Hills.* Greenwillow Books, 1992.

Lambert, David. *Our World: Grasslands.* Silver Burdett Press, 1989.

Siebert, Diane. *Heartland.* Thomas Y. Crowell, 1989.

Siy, Alexandra. *Native Grasslands.* Dillon Press, 1991.

Stone, Lynn. *EcoZones: Prairies.* Rourke Enterprises, 1988.

Taylor, Dave. *Endangered Grassland Animals.* Crabtree Publishing Company, 1992.

Desert Regions

Amsel, Sheri. *Deserts.* Raintree Steck-Vaughn, 1992.

Baker, Lucy. *Life in the Deserts.* Franklin Watts, 1990.

Bash, Barbara. *Desert Giant: The World of the Saguaro Cactus.* Little, Brown and Company, 1989.

George, Michael. *Deserts.* Creative Education, 1992.

Guiberson, Brenda. *Cactus Hotel.* Henry Holt and Company, 1991.

Lerner, Carol. *A Desert Year.* Morrow Junior Books, 1991.

Lye, Keith. *Our World: Deserts.* Silver Burdett, 1987.

Norden, Carroll. *Deserts.* Raintree Steck-Vaughn, 1987.

Simon, Seymour. *Deserts.* Morrow Junior Books, 1990.

Stone, Lynn. *Deserts.* Rourke Enterprises, 1989.

Bibliography

Twist, Clint. *Ecology Watch: Deserts.* Dillon Press, 1991.

Watts, Barrie. *Twenty-four Hours in a Desert.* Franklin Watts, 1991.

Williams, Lawrence. *Last Frontiers for Mankind: Deserts.* Marshall Cavendish, 1990.

Seashore Regions

Chinery, Michael. *Ocean Animals.* Random House, 1992.

George, Jean Craighead. *The Moon of the Deer.* HarperCollins, 1992.

Gibbons, Gail. *Surrounded by Sea: Life on a New England Fishing Island.* Little Brown and Company, 1991.

Jonas, Ann. *Reflections.* Greenwillow Books, 1987.

Lye, Keith. *Our World: Coasts.* Silver Burdett Press, 1989.

Pope, Joyce. *Seashores.* Troll Associates, 1990.

Simon, Seymour. *Oceans.* Morrow Junior Books, 1990.

Stone, Lynn. *EcoZones: Seashores.* Rourke Enterprises, 1988.

Thaxter, Celia. *Celia's Island Journal.* Little, Brown and Company, 1992.

Watts, Barrie. *Twenty-four Hours on a Seashore.* Franklin Watts, 1990.

Zolotow, Charlotte. *The Seashore Book.* HarperCollins, 1992.

Mountain Regions

Amsel, Sheri. *Habitats of the World: Mountains.* Raintree Steck-Vaughn, 1992.

Burbank, Jonathan. *Cultures of the World: Nepal.* Marshall Cavendish, 1991.

Dionetti, Michelle. *Coal Mine Peaches.* Orchard Books, 1991.

Houston, Gloria. *The Year of the Perfect Christmas Tree: An Appalachian Story.* Dial Books, 1988.

Kent, Deborah. *America the Beautiful: Pennsylvania.* Childrens Press, 1988.

Rylant, Cynthia. *Appalachia: The Voices of Sleeping Birds.* Harcourt Brace Jovanovich, 1991.

Siebert, Diane. *Sierra.* HarperCollins, 1991.

Stone, Lynn. *Mountains.* Rourke Enterprises, 1989.

Taylor, Dave. *Endangered Mountain Animals.* Crabtree Publishing Company, 1992.

Thompson, Kathleen. *Portrait of America: West Virginia.* Raintree Steck Vaughan, 1988.

Polar Regions

Aldis, Rodney. *Ecology Watch: Polar Lands.* Dillon Press, 1992.

Byles, Monica. *Life in the Polar Lands.* Franklin Watts, 1990.

Carr, Terry. *Spill! The Story of the Exxon Valdez.* Franklin Watts, 1991.

Cowcher, Helen. *Antarctica.* Farrar Straus and Giroux, 1990.

DeArmond, Dale. *The Seal Oil Lamp.* Little, Brown and Company, 1988.

Ekoomiak, Normee. *Arctic Memories.* Henry Holt and Company, 1992.

Kalman, Bobbie. *The Arctic Land.* Crabtree Publishing Company, 1988.

Kendall, Russ. *Eskimo Boy: Life in an Inupiaq Eskimo Village.* Scholastic, 1992.

LaBonte, Gail. *The Arctic Fox.* Dillon Press, 1989.

Stone, Lynn. *EcoZones: Arctic Tundra.* Rourke Enterprises, 1988.

Williams, Lawrence. *Last Frontiers for Mankind: Polar Lands.* Marshall Cavendish, 1990.

World Cultures

Baillie, Allan, and Chun-Chan Yeh. *Bawshou Rescues the Sun.* Scholastic, 1991. (China)

Bruchac, Joseph, and Jonathan London. *Thirteen Moons on Turtle's Back: A Native American Year of Moons.* Philomel Books, 1992. (Native American)

Bibliography

Caduto, Michael J., and Joseph Bruchac. *Keepers of the Animals: Native American Stories and Wildlife Activities for Children.* Fulcrum Publishing, 1991.

———. *Keepers of the Earth: Native American Stories and Environmental Activities for Children.* Fulcrum Publishing, 1988.

Chiasson, John. *African Journey.* Bradbury Press, 1987.

DeArmond, Dale. *The Seal Oil Lamp.* Little, Brown and Company, 1988. (Native American)

De Paola, Tomie. *The Legend of the Indian Paintbrush.* G.P. Putnam's Sons, 1991. (Native American)

Fisher, Leonard Everett. *Calendar Art: Thirteen Days, Weeks, Months, Years from Around the World.* Macmillan, 1987.

George, Jean Craighead. *One Day in the Tropical Rain Forest.* HarperCollins, 1990. (Venezuela)

Gerson, Mary-Joan. *Why the Sky Is Far Away: A Nigerian Folktale.* Little, Brown and Company, 1992.

Goodman, Jim. *Cultures of the World: Thailand.* Marshall Cavendish, 1991.

Hamilton, Virginia. *Drylongso.* Harcourt Brace Jovanovich, 1992. (United States)

———. *In the Beginning: Creation Stories from Around the World.* Harcourt Brace Jovanovich, 1988.

Haskins, Jim. *Count Your Way Through China.* Carolrhoda Books, 1987.

———. *Count Your Way Through Germany.* Carolrhoda Books, 1990.

Hudson, Wade. *Pass It On: African-American Poetry for Children.* Scholastic, 1993.

Isadora, Rachel. *Over the Green Hills.* Greenwillow Books, 1992. (Africa)

Lewin, Ted. *Amazon Boy.* Macmillan, 1993. (South America)

Lopez, Barry. *Crow and Weasel.* North Point Press, 1990. (Native American)

Luenn, Nancy. *Song for the Ancient Forest.* Atheneum, 1993. (United States)

McDermott, Gerald. *Raven: A Trickster Tale from the Pacific Northwest.* Harcourt Brace Jovanovich, 1993. (Native American)

Mirpuri, Gouri. *Cultures of the World: Indonesia.* Marshall Cavendish, 1991.

Mollel, Tololwa. *A Promise to the Sun: A Story of Africa.* Little, Brown and Company, 1992.

Munan, Heidi. *Cultures of the World: Malaysia.* Marshall Cavendish, 1991.

Osborne, Mary Pope. *Mermaid Tales From Around the World.* Scholastic, 1993.

Palacios, Argentina. *Viva Mexico! A Story of Benito Juarez and Cinco de Mayo.* Raintree Steck-Vaughn, 1992. (Mexico)

Reilly, Mary Jo. *Cultures of the World: Mexico.* Marshall Cavendish, 1991.

Rose, Deborah Lee. *The People Who Hugged the Trees.* Robert Rinehart, 1990. (India)

San Souci, Robert. *Cut from the Same Cloth: American Women of Myth, Legend and Tall Tale.* Philomel Books, 1993.

Sheppard, Nancy. *Alitji in Dreamland.* Ten Speed Press, 1992. (Australia)

Tejima, Keizaburo. *Ho-Limlim: A Rabbit Tale from Japan.* Philomel Books, 1990.

Tope, Lily Rose. *Cultures of the World: Philippines.* Marshall Cavendish, 1991.

Wanasundera, Nanda. *Cultures of the World: Sri Lanka.* Marshall Cavendish, 1991.

Waters, Kate. *Sarah Morton's Day: A Day in the Life of a Pilgrim Girl.* Scholastic, 1989. (United States)

Wells, Rosemary. *Waiting for the Evening Star.* Dial, 1993. (United States)

Bibliography

The Earth's Elements

Baker, Jeannie. *Window*. Greenwillow Books, 1991.

Bannan, Jan Gumprecht. *Sand Dunes*. Carolrhoda Books, 1989.

Barrett, Ian. *Tundra and People*. Silver Burdett Company, 1982.

Baylor, Byrd. *The Way to Start a Day*. Aladdin Books, 1986.

Bianchi, John, and Frank B. Edwards. *Snow: Learning for the Fun of It*. Bungalo Books, 1992.

Bruchac, Joseph, and Jonathan London. *The Thirteen Moons on Turtle's Back: A Native American Year of Moons*. Philomel, 1992.

Cobb, Vicki. *Why Doesn't the Earth Fall Up? And Other Not Such Dumb Questions about Motion*. EP Dutton, 1988.

Conley, Andrea. *Window on the Deep: The Adventures of Underwater Explorer Sylvia Earle*. Franklin Watts, 1991.

Cooney, Barbara. *Miss Rumphius*. Viking, 1982.

Frasier, Debra. *On the Day You Were Born*. Harcourt Brace Jovanovich, 1991.

George, Jean Craighead. *One Day in the Alpine Tundra*. Thomas Y. Crowell, 1984.

George, Michael. *The Moon*. The Child's World Inc, 1992.

———. *The Moon*. Creative Education Inc, 1993.

Hare, Tony. *The Ozone Layer*. Gloucester Press, 1990.

Killion, Bette. *The Same Wind*. Laura Geringer Books; Imprint of HarperCollins, 1992.

Kitchen, Bert. *Somewhere Today*. Candlewick Press, 1992.

Knight, Margy Burns. *Talking Walls*. Tilbury House, 1992.

Lambert, David. *Our World: Seas and Oceans*. Silver Burdett Press, 1987.

Lopez, Barry. *Crow and Weasel*. North Point Press, 1990.

McConnell, Anita. *The World Beneath Us*. Facts on File Inc, 1985.

Mollel, Totolwa M. *A Promise to the Sun: A Story of Africa*. Little, Brown and Company, 1992.

Morimoto, Junko. *My Hiroshima*. Viking, 1990.

Murphy, Bryan. *Experiment with Water*. Lerner Publications Company, 1991.

Myers, Lynne B., and Christopher A. Myers. *McCrephy's Field*. Houghton Mifflin, 1991.

Pechter, Alese, and Morton Pechter. *What's in the Deep? An Underwater Adventure for Children*. Acropolis Books, 1991.

Pringle, Laurence. *Global Warming: Assessing the Greenhouse Threat*. Arcade Publishing, 1990.

Schmid, Eleonore. *The Air Around Us*. North-South Books, 1992.

Simon, Seymour. *Icebergs and Glaciers*. William Morrow & Co, Inc, 1987.

Souza, D. M. *Powerful Waves*. Carolrhoda Books, 1992.

Steele, Philip. *Wind: Causes and Effects*. Franklin Watts, 1991.

Taylor, Ron. *The Invisible World*. Facts on File Inc, 1986.

Walker, Jane. *Natural Disasters: Avalanches and Landslides*. Gloucester Press, 1992.

Walker, Sally M. *Water Up, Water Down: The Hydrologic Cycle*. Carolrhoda Books, 1992.

Whitfield, Philip, and Joyce Pope. *Why Do The Seasons Change?* Viking Kestral, 1987.

Yolen, Jane. *Encounter*. Harcourt Brace Jovanovich, 1992.